KEYNSHAM & SALTFORD

1945 - 2020

Edited by Richard Dyson

**Keynsham & Saltford
Local History Society**

BRISTOL BOOKS

Bristol Books CIC, The Courtyard, Wraxall,
Wraxall Hill, Bristol, BS48 1NA

Keynsham & Saltford: 1945-2020
Written and researched by members of
Keynsham & Saltford Local History Society.

Published by Bristol Books 2020

ISBN: 978-1-909446-25-0

Front cover images are courtesy of Keynsham &
Saltford Local History Society (upper) & Dr Sarah
Fox (lower).

By the White Hart, about 1966

CONTENTS

PART I – THROUGH THE YEARS

Springtime at Fry's, 1952

FOREWORD

The idea for this book arose when the Society's Committee discussed how we should mark our fiftieth anniversary – that was back in 2015. A comprehensive history of the area up to 1945 was published in 1990, so we decided to bring that up to date. Society members and others formed a group and together they have researched newspapers, existing publications, archives and probed local memories to find the raw material and write sections. Completion has been delayed by other Society projects, but 2020 has proved to be a good year to set as an end point, marking 75 years since the end of the Second World War.

When we started, our idea was to compile a chronological account of the period and this forms the first part, using a selection of events. It soon became clear, however, that this snapshot approach could not cover everything, so we extended our reach to include a section on people of interest who have a local connection, sports clubs and aspects of life that affect us all, such as shops, schools and transport.

Whilst we have set boundaries at each end of the period, where it is helpful we have reached back to give a short history of institutions including Keynsham Hospital and Fry's. It is impossible to cover all aspects of life in one small volume and there are many noteworthy individuals, events, businesses and voluntary organizations that are not mentioned. Keynsham and Saltford together have a remarkable number of social activities, societies, sports groups and charities; I hope we have covered enough to give a flavour of local life, even if your favourite does not get a mention.

I must take this opportunity to thank all those who have helped to make this book see the light of day. They are too numerous to name but the Committee of the Society has been most supportive, our researchers and authors have made it possible, whilst individuals in many organizations both locally and further afield have provided information, text, illustrations and permissions.

I am writing this in the lockdown period imposed as a result of the coronavirus epidemic, which is proving to have the greatest impact on everyday life of any event since 1945. It is too soon to include a description of the effects locally, but perhaps this will form the first chapter in the next book on our local history. In the meantime, whether you are a native of Keynsham or Saltford, a more recent arrival like me, or a newcomer, I hope you will find plenty of enjoyment in these pages and I'm sure you will learn some things you didn't know.

Richard Dyson

Chairman
Keynsham & Saltford Local History Society

PART I
THROUGH THE YEARS

1945
VE DAY

8May 1945 was VE (Victory in Europe) Day, the day following the formal military surrender of Nazi Germany after nearly six years of war. Fighting against Japan was still in progress but the day was declared a public holiday for celebration across Britain. The end of the War had been expected so there had been a few days in which to plan events and parties.

Children pose in St Anne's Avenue, Keynsham on VE Day

Events included a concert at the Drill Hall on Bath Hill

1945-1948
AFTER THE WAR

For five-and-a-half long years, all the resources and energy of the nation had been ploughed into winning the Second World War. Months before VE Day it was known that the surrender of Nazi Germany was just a matter of time and planning for the peace was well underway. Nonetheless, the transition from a war-based economy, with the essentials of life rationed and government control of industry and commerce, to a normal civilian world was an enormous undertaking and would take years to bring about.

It is difficult to find detailed facts about how this transition was managed in Keynsham and Saltford but we have drawn on the minutes of Keynsham Urban District Council and its committees to give a flavour of some of the problems and changes at that time.

June and September 1945
Evacuation Scheme

Throughout the War, the Council had received regular reports on the numbers currently accommodated in the area under the Government Evacuation Scheme. In September 1944 the number officially billeted had been 409, with another 125 "expected soon" as a result of the V2 rocket attacks. The numbers then fell quickly.

Number officially billeted in district	at 31 May 1945	at 5 Sept 1945
Mothers and Children	94	78
Unaccompanied Children	20	4
Others	9	2
Total	123	84

August 1945
Hamleaze Sick Bay

The Ministry of Health has decided to discontinue use of the Sick Bay [which in April 1944 had eight staff and eight patients] and it is to be closed as soon as possible. Staff will be given one month's notice.

October 1945
Fuel Economy

A letter has been received from the Ministry of Fuel and Power requesting the "greatest possible economies" in the use of fuel by the Council.

November 1945 and February 1946
War-time Nursery School

Somerset County Council intend to close the war-time Nursery School at Ellsbridge House. The Urban District Council need to know what the demand is. The report received in February said that 150 children needed to be catered for, so the operation needed to be bigger, not closed down. The school stayed open.

February 1946
Gifts of Food

Four cases of foodstuffs had been received from the City of Melbourne for distribution to aged and needy persons. To be distributed at the British Restaurant on 11 February.

June 1946
Blast Walls

Tenders have been invited for the removal of all blast walls in Keynsham but no quotes have been received.

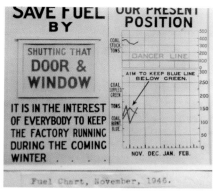

Publicity encouraging economy in the use of fuel at Fry's in 1946

April 1946

World Food Situation

In response to a letter from the Prime Minister, the following actions were agreed:

- Charlton Cinema to be requested to show a suitable slide emphasizing the urgent need for the utmost economy in the use of bread and other cereals.
- Application to be made to obtain posters to be displayed on Council notice boards, bakers' shops and at suitable points in as many streets as possible. The Ministry of Food to be requested to increase advertising at national level so as to display larger posters in the Council area.

June 1946

Gas Masks

The Council had been asked what people should do with the gas masks distributed to everyone in September 1939. They referred the query to the County Council who said there is no organization for collecting these respirators and the Home Secretary had said in Parliament on 6 December 1945 that the public should keep them in case they are needed again.

June 1947

Air Raid Shelter on Bath Hill

An application had been received to use the shelter for growing mushrooms by an up-to-date manure-less process. Permission was refused as the Council wish to remove all Air Raid Protection works at the earliest possible date.

December 1947

Welfare Food

Letter received from the Ministry of Food stating that they are prepared to establish a centre for the distribution of welfare foods in the vicinity of the High Street for one half-day per week, provided volunteers carry out the work. Resolved that the Clerk will approach the WRVS and ask for their assistance.

July 1948

Royal Electrical and Mechanical Engineers (REME)

The Clerk reported that Major Playfair, Commanding Officer of the REME unit at Wellsway, had told him that the unit would be leaving the District in August and it is his wish to have an opportunity for the unit to express its appreciation of the happy circumstances that had at all times attended their sojourn in the District.

13

1946
LOCAL ADVERTISEMENTS

A year or so after the War, Keynsham Urban District Council authorized a town guide with the cost offset by advertising. Below is a selection of the adverts – straightforward, with no graphics and in black and white, reflecting the austerity and rationing then prevailing.

Telephone 3272

Edward Wiggins

BUILDER, DECORATOR
—AND—
GENERAL CONTRACTOR

CONTRACTS NET (DUE ON COMPLETION)
ESTIMATES FREE

KELSTON HOUSE, HIGH STREET
KEYNSHAM

CULVERHAY SCHOOL

FOR JUNIOR GIRLS & BOYS
to 11 years of age
AND KINDERGARTEN

2, THE PARK,   KEYNSHAM
NR. BRISTOL

Principal : CHRYSTABEL COOKSLEY
L.R.A.M. Eloc. L.G.S.M. Eloc.

PROSPECTUS ON APPLICATION   TEL. KEYNSHAM 2228

MILLS & MILLS

DISPENSING CHEMISTS
37 HIGH STREET
KEYNSHAM
Telephone 2148

Hours of Attendance
Weekdays : 9 a.m. - 7 p.m.
Wednesdays : 9 a.m. - 1 p.m.
7 p.m. - 7.30 p.m.
SUNDAYS : 12 - 1 p.m. 7 - 7.30 p.m.
OXYGEN ALWAYS IN READINESS

TELEPHONE 2170

E. G. WILLIAMS

Grocer, Greengrocer and
Provision Merchant

High Street

Saltford

A PERSONAL SERVICE SHOP   Member of the I.T.A.

WILLOUGHBY BROS.

High-Class Grocers and Provision Merchants

North Somerset Supply Stores

KEYNSHAM

TELEPHONE - 3154

ESTABLISHED OVER HALF A CENTURY

Telephone: KEYNSHAM 3268

Herbert W. G. Belsten
(L. J. GUYAN)

Carpenter, Builder
and Funeral Director

14 Charlton Road - KEYNSHAM
Near Bristol

TELEPHONE 2254

W. COOPER & SON

Builders, Decorators,
Shopfitters and
Sanitary Engineers

Highgrove Street, Totterdown, Bristol, 4
And at
WEST VIEW ROAD, KEYNSHAM

Phone: SALTFORD 3205

WALTER BATSTONE

High-Class Baker
and Confectioner

Saltford Bakery - SALTFORD
Nr. BRISTOL

1948
SALTFORD ROMAN COFFIN

Routine building and agricultural activities occasionally throw up an unexpected and exciting find. Such an event happened at Saltford on 15 September 1948, whilst workmen were removing a stump of an elm tree in a field about 500 yards to the south of Manor Road, west of the lane up to Gypsy Lane/Ashton Hill. After striking hard material, they uncovered a stone slab which proved to be the cover of a Roman coffin.

Careful excavation exposed the whole coffin and the cover stone, although damaged by tree roots, was lifted. Inside the coffin was a skeleton. The police, the Somerset Archaeology Society and the local Speleological Society were informed and the grave and skeleton were photographed. After removal for expert examination, the skeleton was found to be of a healthy young man, about 21 years of age.

A detailed description of the coffin was made. It had been cut from a single block of Bath oolite stone, probably from Box or Corsham, and hollowed out. Externally, the base had been shaped like a barrel to enable it to be lowered with a rocking motion, in spite of its great weight, with ease into the grave. The cover stone had been bedded on a thin layer of yellow sand mortar.

It was buried in a grave about 11ft x 8ft (3.5m x 2.4m), with the top about 2'-6" (0.8m) below the surface. The base was roughly paved with stones bedded in blue clay, and sloped so that it drained well. After the coffin had been positioned, walls of rough stone had been built up round it, with the stones embedded in blue clay. The alignment was north to south, with the head to the north.

Pieces of pottery, fragments of stone tiles, rusted nails, and oyster shells were also found around the burial site, suggesting that there had been Roman occupation nearby.

The coffin was removed from the site and placed in the garden at Wick House Farm, of which the field was part. For many years it was used as a plant container, but eventually it was removed and is believed to have been dumped elsewhere in Saltford. So, the whereabouts of this important fragment of local archaeology is no longer known.

1949
WHERE WE WORKED

L ate in 1949, a detailed report was presented to local councillors containing information on the local area and its population. This included figures on the types of work people had within Keynsham and Saltford and numbers employed in local industrial businesses. The tables give a snapshot of employment at the time. (People travelling to work elsewhere are not included.)

Employment in the principal categories (excluding professional and administrative)

	Women Employed	Men Employed	Total Employed
Agriculture	20	150	170
Retail and Distribution	90	172	262
Engineering and Industry	1,140	1,672	2,812
Building Trades	0	107	107
Hotels, Restaurants, Entertainment	30	23	53
Domestic Helps	67	1	68
Railways	2	31	33

Local industrial employers with more than five employees - number of staff.

	Type of Business	Women Employed	Men Employed	Total Employed
Fry's	Chocolate Manufacture	1,034	1,385	2,419
ES & A Robinson	Envelopes & Letterheads	63	33	96
ES & A Robinson	Paper-making	10	86	96
Polysulphin	Washing Powders & Soaps	0	43	43
Reynolds Brothers	Dairy Produce	4	22	26
Taylors Paints (Saltford)	Paint Manufacture	8	13	21
Somerset Pickle Factory	Pickle & Vinegar Maker	10	4	14
L A Dunn	Body and Car Builders	1	11	12
Barton Motors	Light Engineering	0	11	11
Somerdale Motor Co	Motor Engineers	0	7	7
Gould Thomas & Co [Albert Mill]	Dry Salters & Chemical Factors	1	6	7
Keeling & Sons	Cement & Waterproofers	1	6	7
J D Products Ltd	Rug & Carpet Makers	6	1	7
EA Cannock	General Repairs	0	6	6
St Keyna Motor Works	Motor Engineers	1	5	6
Throsper Engineering	Tool-making	1	5	6

The illustrations show people at work locally a couple of years later.

The photographs contrast the conditions at Albert Mill, with the chemicals used in producing dyestuffs and probably little changed in the preceding fifty years, with those at the modern Fry's Somerdale factory. All were taken in the same year – 1951.

Albert Mill - the glauber salt tanks

Albert Mill - drawing off acetic acid

Fry's P Block, engineering machine shop

Fry's B Block, cream tablet wrapping

1951
KEYNSHAM FESTIVAL OF BRITAIN

I n the summer of 1951, the Festival of Britain was a national exhibition and fair held in London; for a nation that had suffered years of war and austerity it was a chance to celebrate and enjoy the inventiveness and creativity of our scientists and technologists. The Festival inspired communities across the country to do something similar and in Keynsham a mini-Festival was organized. An "At Home" event included pony rides, a flower auction, sideshows and refreshment stalls; dances were held at the Women's Institute hut and by the Young Conservatives; a party of Dutch visitors was entertained. However, it was Mary Fairclough and the Keynsham and Saltford Arts Club who rose to the occasion and provided the centrepiece of the programme with an imaginative Keynsham Festival Exhibition that ran from 16 to 21 June.

The original idea was an exhibition of Arts and Crafts but it evolved into a display that combined this with an historical theme that led to many older pieces of local craft work being included. These were lent by individuals and businesses from around the district.

Arts and crafts embraced a wide range of activities including book-binding, smocking, sculpture, leatherwork and weaving as well as the painting, embroidery and woodwork that one might find today. Historical items were entered under the heading of "Old Keynsham".

Rural crafts were represented by saddlery, a wheelwright's display and basketwork. Blacksmith Bob Trott submitted a variety of horseshoes he had made over the years, including some for hunters and race-horses, with some very old double-shoes dating from the time when oxen ploughed the fields. Another unusual item from earlier times on the farm was an old harvest field "lowance" jug, which held 49 pints, and was used to refresh the thirsty reapers during harvest.

Fry's contributed a large exhibit of interesting items including a pestle and mortar once belonging to Anna Fry, head of the business in 1787, and the sample box used by the first of the company's commercial travellers. Examples of gowns and dresses up to a hundred years old were displayed, while ancient history was represented by a mosaic found at Somerdale and a model of the Roman Villa found on the site.

The exhibition was held at the Fear Institute on the High Street and was opened by Colonel Dainton, Chairman of Keynsham Urban District Council, with a speech that was reported in full in the Bath Weekly Chronicle.

To accompany the exhibition a ten-page booklet was written by Mary Fairclough, giving a detailed account of the history of Keynsham. The event was very popular and there are good grounds for thinking that it was this exhibition, together with the booklet, that first made people realise that Keynsham had a history worth discovering and documenting.

The whole Festival was a great success; this extended to the finances. A copy of the accounts exists and income from all events totalled £97 13s 7d against expenses of £33 18s 5d.

| 8 APRIL | The National Census recorded the population of Keynsham Urban District as 8,277, of which 1,928 were recorded as living in Saltford. |

Exhibits – weaving and cabinet-making

Visitors browse among the exhibits

Modelling exhibits included some fine pieces of precision engineering

1952
MEMORIAL PARK OPENED

n 1947, Keynsham Urban District Council (KUDC) bought a section of the old Abbey precinct to create a park in the centre of Keynsham as a lasting memorial to the fallen of the two world wars. The next few years saw various plans produced for the development of this and work soon started on the first phase.

> The Domesday Survey of 1086 records six mills in Keynsham and the remains of one of these, Abbey or Downe Mill, survive on the River Chew at the east side of the park. Originally a grist mill used for grinding corn, it was later used as a brass mill, then as part of a manufacturing process for emery and glass paper and latterly as a colour mill producing pigments for paint. Production continued (by the Valley Watermills Colour Company) up to and through the Second World War, preparing colour bases for camouflage paint. Work ceased at the end of the war, the buildings being demolished in 1952, but the weir and sluice gates remain. The waterwheel was rescued from a derelict mill in the Chew Valley and installed in 1968.

The Colour Mill and Cottages, about 1950

Significant work was involved in raising the ground level on the east side of the Chew and material from the demolition of the wartime blast walls and clinker brought from Wick was used for this. On the opposite side, a further 13 acres were bought in 1949 to extend the site and work included grading the slope and installing tennis courts. The War Memorial gates were erected early in 1952 and after further groundworks, the park was opened on 10 August 1952. The Memorial Gates were dedicated to the memory of the 129 local men listed, who lost their lives in both world wars, by the Vicar of St John's, Rev Trevor Wright.

By the early 1960s, a bowling green had been added to the facilities on offer and a stylish and award-winning bandstand erected on the bank of the River Chew. A less picturesque addition was the 150 ft (46 m) span reinforced concrete bridge over the lower end of the park – erected in 1966 to carry the by-pass. In 1967 the Council's Highways and Parks Committee allowed free fishing for all in the lower park, with the Keynsham Angling Association retaining exclusive rights at the north end. The floods of 1968 left the park in a sorry state and the damage caused took a year to rectify, with the work being carried out alongside the extension of the park to the south after the UDC bought more land at Dapps Hill, previously the site of The Pines and Grove Cottage.

The park was further extended in 1971 following the demolition of Fairfield Terrace, the Mission Chapel and Woodbine Steps, with riverside paths created and lighting installed throughout. The overall design and layout of this extension was the work of the renowned landscape architect Dame Sylvia Crowe, who designed the rose garden at the Oxford Botanic Gardens among many other public spaces.

The 1980s saw a surge of vandalism in the park which resulted in the bandstand being badly damaged but development of the public

A view of the Memorial Park in the 1950s

space continued with the creation of a scented garden for the visually impaired and a BMX cycle track at the bottom of Bath Hill for younger residents. This facility was withdrawn in 1988 when it made way for the creation of a car park.

Work in the lower park in the 1990s saw alterations to the lake, with a new pumping station, and the subsequent landscaping now provides a home for the Keynsham crocodile. Following years of damage and neglect it was decided to replace the bandstand with a new structure and canopy in 2007 and a skateboard park was also added beyond the now upgraded tennis courts. The Keynsham mosaics, which had been created by the community under the guidance of artist Roz Waters to celebrate the Millennium, were relocated in the park as part of the regeneration of the Town Hall area. Here they joined the sundial created in 2007 by the Junior Gateway Summer Play scheme, which involved over thirty children.

Improvements to the park and its facilities continued with the installation of an outdoor gym along the east side of the River Chew in 2015, which was also the first year that the park won a Gold Award in the RHS Britain In Bloom competition. Memorial Park is also a winner of the Green Flag Award which recognizes the best parks and green spaces in the country. In 2020, the park continues to provide leisure and sporting facilities for the whole community; it provides a central focal point and performance area for the Keynsham Music Festival as well as hosting musical events throughout the summer months.

The original bandstand seen in 1975

21

1953
CORONATION CELEBRATIONS

The coronation of Queen Elizabeth II took place at Westminster Abbey on 2 June 1953, sixteen months after the death of her father King George VI. The period of mourning and then preparation enabled a lavish programme of celebrations to be arranged across the country and the Commonwealth.

Locally, a Keynsham and Saltford Coronation Committee was set up and arranged a nine-day programme of events suitable for all ages and involving many voluntary groups.

Residents were invited to donate towards Coronation memorials in the form of trees, shrubs and seats. Services were held at Keynsham Parish Church, the Baptist Church and St Dunstan's Church and throughout the week the Parish Church was floodlit at night.

Children under sixteen received a Coronation mug and could enter competitions for handwriting, picture or poster, art, handicraft, sewing or knitting. Shopkeepers took part in a window-dressing competition. Fancy-dress parades were held in both Keynsham and Saltford. Older residents were treated to Coronation teas. Keynsham Hospital was decorated, a festive tea provided and patients presented with a commemorative rosette and handkerchief.

Coronation Day, following the solemnity of the church services, was celebrated with street parties, followed by an evening of fun at the Crown Ground. There were side-shows, light refreshments and a programme of events: a crazy football match, musical chairs on bicycles, old time and square dancing, a short religious service, choral and community singing and fireworks - all rounded off at midnight by the singing of the National Anthem. During the evening Coronation bonfires were lit on Stantonbury Hill.

Official Programme of Keynsham & Saltford Coronation Celebrations ER II

During the extended celebrations, there were dances, whist drives at the British Legion, a treasure hunt organised by the Young Conservatives, and Keynsham Cricket Club played special matches. Other events included performances by the Drama Section of the Arts Club, a Saltford WI supper and a Festival Week at Saltford Golf Club. Many buildings in both Saltford and Keynsham were decorated for the celebrations.

A lasting commemoration remains in the road names Coronation Avenue and Queens Road in the housing development in southwest Keynsham that was under construction at the time.

Shops at the top of Bath Hill were decorated for the occasion

One special feature of the Coronation was that it was televised. It was the first major event that people could watch in their own homes – provided they could afford to buy a television set. We don't know how many local people were able to follow the ceremony at home or with neighbours but sales of the small (a 14-inch screen was normal) black and white sets went up everywhere. It is said that on average each one was watched by ten people. By today's standards the pictures they saw were poor quality and the sets very expensive, typically costing £1,000 to £2,000 at 2020 prices, with only one channel (BBC). One of the few places they could be obtained locally was at Ivan Strudwick's electrical shop at 53 High Street.

Fancy Dress at Culvers Road/Cranmore Avenue

31 MARCH   From this date the Council banned all grazing on the land purchased for the future extension of Keynsham Memorial Park.

1956
WELLSWAY SCHOOL OPENED

These were the first pupils to enter Wellsway County Secondary School in 1956. In the centre are Mrs Nicholls, Miss Burridge, Miss Laramy (now Ellison), Headmaster Mr Melborne and Mr Whistlecroft

It is seldom that two new schools begin their lives in one building but on 10 September 1956 this happened in Keynsham: Keynsham Grammar School and Wellsway County Secondary School were opened.

The intake, all first years [what would now be Year 7], comprised 71 Grammar School pupils and 90 Wellsway County Secondary pupils. Some of the Grammar pupils came from Bathampton, Bathford and Batheaston, as these were part of the County of Somerset which was the local education authority, the City of Bath being a separate authority.

The uniform for the Grammar School pupils was navy and light blue and for the Wellsway pupils it was grey and green.

The first headteacher was Mr Melborne, who was temporarily in charge of both schools until the appointment of Mr Jack Skinner to the Grammar School in 1958. Officially, both schools were opened in 1957; the Grammar School by Sir Graham Savage and the Wellsway School by Ted Leather, the local MP. The photograph shows the first of these events on 4 October 1957.

The two schools shared the same building and members of staff for two years, with lessons taught in separate areas but other activities combined. The gymnasium was not completed for several weeks and there were no playing fields for the first year. A walk to Manor Road Playing Fields was necessary for winter games lessons but the playground was used for netball and other activities as well as the school hall. A start was made in that first year on digging a swimming pool but this was never completed: an open-air pool was built in the 1970s and later covered, using funds raised by the Parent-

Work nears completion, about 1957

The opening of Keynsham Grammar School on 4 October 1957

Teacher Association.

In 1958, after further construction work, Wellsway County Secondary School moved to its own building further up the driveway; the block later known as Mendip. The building which had been shared remained as the Grammar School; this later became the Lansdown building.

The two schools were eventually amalgamated in 1971 when Wellsway Comprehensive was formed; this also brought about a change in catchment boundaries. Lansdown block was used for the younger pupils and Mendip for the older ones. Local government re-organization in 1974 saw further administrative changes with responsibility moving from Somerset County Council to the newly formed County of Avon.

Over the years the school has expanded greatly with the 1990s seeing a new art block constructed at the front of the building and the sixth-form block added to the Mendip building. More recently a new gym and other buildings have been added, and in 2016 the IKB Studio School was built on the site. Wellsway became an Academy in 2011, so that it is no longer under local authority control.

1958
ENGLAND'S OLDEST HOUSE

The year 1958 was not of particular significance in the long history of Saltford Manor. But it was very significant in the knowledge of this history and awareness of the manor's existence. On 24 July 1958 the magazine Country Life published a very detailed four-page article on the history of Saltford Manor, including a dozen photographs. We have a copy of the article, written by Bryan Little, a lecturer at the University of Bristol. He was an expert and a prolific author on architectural history, especially in the south-west of England.

Mr Little believed that - castles and palaces apart - Saltford Manor has a good claim to be the oldest dwelling-place in England. Of course, this is the sort of record for which there might well be a great deal of competition, but the article made a good case for his belief. In 2003, the manor did win a contest to find the oldest continuously inhabited house in England.

The building we see today, next to St Mary's Church, has been greatly altered over the centuries. It would originally have had only two storeys and at its heart the original Norman house, probably built between 1120 and 1166, was a simple rectangle in plan; most of its walls remain, although the space within has been sub-divided. One of many distinctive features, on the north side, is a Norman window which would once have lit the main hall, although it now opens onto the master bedroom. Another is the remains of wall paintings, probably from the thirteenth century: the subjects have been identified as the *Virgin and Child* and the *Wheel of Fortune*, the latter being the only known English example of this in a domestic setting.

Over the centuries, ownership of the Manor House – and indeed its name – has changed many times. The longest continuous owner was the Flower family who bought a share of it in 1627, later bought the rest and kept the property until it was sold by Noel Flower in 1946 for £900.

1960
KEYNSHAM RE-BUILDING BEGINS

Looking across Bath Hill West. All the houses in the background were demolished.

F ive months after it was established in 1938, Keynsham UDC decided "to obtain the services of a private architect to prepare a scheme for the provision of public offices on a site in Bath Hill East. A self-contained administrative building is a pressing need... and it is hoped that speedy progress will be made". By any standards the accommodation for the Council's staff was inadequate; the offices were situated near the bottom of Wellsway and although minor extensions were made there was no space for a sizeable building to accommodate increasing staff numbers. Council meetings were held upstairs at the former Liberal Club on Bath Hill.

The war delayed all such plans but between 1946 and 1958 various proposals were considered. In 1951 it was recommended that a new Civic Centre be built, including post office and library, as well as council chambers and offices. Several sites were considered with the most suitable felt to be at the northern end of Keynsham Park, where the unsurfaced car-

The first part to be completed - seen in 1989

park is in 2020. Approval had to be obtained from central government and, as time moved on, priorities and opinions changed until a final decision was made in 1958 to site the new complex at the top of Bath Hill West.

One of the considerations was probably the need to act on a report from the Sanitary Inspector several years earlier that 139 properties in the Council's area were insanitary and deemed "incapable of repair". They had to be demolished and the inhabitants rehoused. Whilst some of the properties on the five acres

The top of Bath Hill West

Temple Street looking towards the High Street

of land to be redeveloped were sound and of historic or architectural interest, others were poor and covered by the report.

The project required that the whole area be cleared. This meant the disappearance of terraces at The Labbott, Prospect Place and Kelston View, together with their long-established community of residents. In the photograph on the previous page, the building in the centre foreground is almost the only one to survive.

Compulsory purchase took place in 1959-1960 and demolition of the first properties soon followed. As well as houses, several shops had to be demolished so the new centre included two ranks of modern shops in an L-shape. In fact, the new shops were built first and opened in 1961, before the demolition of the buildings near the top of Bath Hill. The corner unit was first occupied by Victor Value, later becoming Tesco, and then Kwik Save.

This development was the first stage in a complete transformation of the Temple Street area; the two pictures are a reminder of some of the old properties that were demolished.

1961
SALTFORD HALL COMPLETED

The Saltford Community Association was formed following a public meeting in July 1949 to discuss the need for a village hall; the first council comprised members representing ten prominent organizations in the village. Fund-raising activities were organised and plans were prepared by Mr Whalley, the architect to Keynsham Urban District Council, for a hall with a capacity of 100-200 people. By 1953, with the building fund at £1,500, fresh plans were drawn up, looking further ahead and allowing extensions according to demand and the availability of funds. These were approved by the Ministry of Education in April 1954, and a grant of £1,500 towards the estimated cost of £4,500 for the construction of the main hall, foyer and cloakrooms was made to the Association. Building commenced immediately, using voluntary labour, and the foundation stone was laid by Lord Hylton, Lord Lieutenant of Somerset, on 11 September 1954.

The amateur workers had to deal with solid rock across much of the site and the slow progress meant that numbers dwindled somewhat. In May 1955, the delivery of twenty tons of precast concrete framework to the site was greeted with delight and gave new impetus to the project. Progress was still slow but the volunteers plodded on. Finally, after ten years of work and fund-raising, reward came on 13 March 1960 when the foyer was opened for use by the village. The tempo of activity now quickened and, coupled with the employment of professionals for roofing, heating and flooring, the main hall was ready to be opened on 13 October 1961 by Lord Hylton, in the presence of the Bishop of Taunton, dignitaries and officials. The final cost was £8,600 but with increased grants and a loan from Somerset County Council the money was found.

In addition to meetings of the regular user organizations and private bookings, the hall hosted the St Mary's Harvest Supper in October, a live broadcast of the BBC's *Any Questions*, and the Annual Horticultural Show. To embellish the main hall, professional artist Alan Durman added the mural above the entrance doors; as well as local landmarks, his wife and dog, he depicted several local villagers including footballer Gordon Mitchell.

By 1964, the building was in constant use and thoughts turned to Phase 2, comprising a

smaller function room, the Avon Room, plus a kitchen and ancillary rooms. This phase was built professionally by EC Thomas of Keynsham and opened in March 1965.

It soon became apparent that a car park was necessary: Keynsham UDC supplied the materials and skilled help, while local residents provided the labour. Tractors and trailers were lent by farmers and builders so that volunteers could remove 300 cubic yards of topsoil. Altogether 107 people, including tea-ladies, took part, with people on morning, afternoon and evening sessions laying ballast, concrete, and fixing fence posts and drains. What an exercise in voluntary self-help and friendship it was!

In 1969, building of the scenery tower above the stage began, plus the three rooms over the foyer and kitchen. The new rooms were officially opened by the Lord Lieutenant of Somerset, who named them 'Somerset' and 'Kelston', while a much-needed office was also provided. The total cost was £14,000 and Somerset County gave a grant of £4,000. As some of the original members of the Association retired, new ones took over, with Gordon Reed as chairman. By 1982, the need for more accommodation was again apparent, so a detached building with its own kitchen and toilets was erected north of the existing kitchen. Wansdyke District Council gave a substantial grant of £18,750 towards a total cost of £30,000, and this building was opened on 13 October 1984 by the Chairman of the Council, Councillor Neville Dove.

Many further improvements have been made since so that, in 2020, the hall continues to be the focus for a thriving Saltford social life and the Community Association that spawned it.

23 APRIL	The National Census was conducted and recorded the population of Keynsham Urban District (which included Saltford) as 15,152 of which 3,044 were recorded as living in Saltford.

1962
KEYNSHAM ARMS GRANTED

On 5 June 1962, Keynsham Urban District Council was formally granted arms. Such a grant, made under Crown authority, follows a very strict process carried out by the College of Arms. Heraldry has precise rules and the language used is unchanged from the Middle Ages, incorporating many French words.

The design would have been developed by the herald's office at the College of Arms, to reflect local history and activities, taking account of suggestions and allusions provided by the Council.

The blazon, or formal description, of the arms is set out in words so that the image can be recreated by any heraldic draughtsman. We have not included this here as the language is hard to understand unless you are an expert. The motto *"Maintien Le Droit"* means "Maintain the Right" or "Uphold the Law", and is that of the Bridges family.

The origin and meaning of the various elements of the arms are as follows:

- The six golden clarions or trumpets on a red background are the arms of the extinct Keynsham Abbey, and the wavy blue and white bars represent the rivers Avon and Chew. Originally, the six clarions came from the arms of the de Clare family who were Earls of Gloucester when the Abbey was founded by William, the second Earl, about 1167.
- The wreath and mantling are in red and gold, the colours of the Abbey arms and also those of Somerset County Council. The Roman crown alludes to the Roman occupation and the golden dragon of Wessex refers both to our Saxon history and to the old brass industry of Keynsham and Saltford. One of the badges of the former "Society of Mineral and Battery Works" was a golden dragon.
- A more specific reference to this formerly important local industry is the brass wire around the dragon's neck, on which is threaded a cogwheel to represent modern industries. Between the dragon's claws is the basic family shield of the Bridges, a reference to their long connection with the district.

When the Council ceased to exist in 1974, the right to use the arms also ended, as this cannot be passed on. The arms are today used by Saltford Golf Club and the clarions and wavy lines form part of the logo of Broadlands Academy, while most of the town's sports clubs make use of the clarions in their emblems or badges.

1963-1964
KEYNSHAM ABBEY RE-DISCOVERED

After Keynsham Abbey was demolished in the sixteenth century the stone was used for other buildings and gradually the site became lost, with the Abbey becoming nothing more than a folk memory. When the houses along Abbey Park were built in Victorian times, various remnants of walls and other remains were dug through; some archaeological work did take place in 1875 but the records and plans made were of limited value.

The general location of the Abbey was known and when land was acquired in 1958 to build the Keynsham by-pass it included the site of much of it: the cloisters and the western end of the nave of the Abbey Church. Advance works started in 1963 and in order to pass beneath Station Road a deep cutting was necessary at this point. All the remaining foundations and any flooring in this area would therefore be completely destroyed. Appalled by the prospect of further unrecorded destruction of Keynsham's heritage, a number of local residents joined a group of volunteers from Bristol Folk House Archaeological Society who had undertaken to literally chase the earth-moving equipment and survey, record, sketch, photograph and rescue as much as possible of the remains that became exposed. It is through their efforts between 1961 and 1966, together with later work, that a partial plan of the lost abbey could be drawn.

The work was meticulously recorded and architectural fragments found enabled much to be learned about the structure and style of building. Further work was carried out in 1975 in the garden of 3 Abbey Park, where the vault believed to have once contained the remains of Jasper Tudor was identified. Then, in 1979, the lines of known walls in the south east corner of the Abbey, where it survives in the corner of the

An exciting moment in the 1979 excavations

These Abbey remains are now overgrown in the by-pass cutting

Memorial Park, were re-excavated. Together with the results of some work done a few years later, we have probably learnt as much as we can from the remains that are currently accessible.

1964-1966
CONSTRUCTION OF THE BY-PASS

Construction of the Bridge over the River Chew in June 1965

The need for a by-pass to take the A4 trunk road around Keynsham was identified in the 1930s and the road was first formally proposed in 1938. A public enquiry was held and the Ministry of Transport considered three routes, deciding on the one eventually adopted. The Second World War delayed the project until 1958, when the route options were reconsidered, with the same outcome.

The scheme progressed through planning and design stages, with the design work and project management undertaken by Somerset County Council as agent for the Ministry of Transport. In early 1964, after tendering, the construction contract for just over £1m was awarded to A E Farr Ltd of Westbury, Wiltshire, who had built several large civil engineering projects in the area including the Chew Valley Reservoir.

With a combination of a crossing over the River Chew and the bridging or closure of several roads the project was a complex one. Routing the dual-carriageway road close to the town centre could not be done without a major impact and preparation involved the compulsory purchase and demolition of several houses, a doctors' surgery and several other buildings of interest. The former National School building on Station Road was a casualty. A strip of land had been reserved between Gaston Avenue and Van Dyck Avenue, and Unity Road was severed. Trees planted to mask the impact on the Memorial Park have now matured but the size of the park and the vista down the river were much diminished by the new road. Excavation for the Station Road

View from the Station Road Bridge in early 1966

cutting destroyed most of what was left of the foundations of Keynsham Abbey.

The main site compound was at the east end of Van Dyck Avenue. After site clearance and fencing the construction comprised two main elements. One was the earthworks, which involved excavating the cutting through Station Road and the west end of the Memorial Park, then using the material from this to build the long embankment across the Hams. A fleet of scrapers and other earth-moving machinery was used but the harder rock lower in the cutting required the use of a large excavator that had to be assembled on site.

Whilst the earthmoving was in progress, work started on the construction of the bridges needed to accommodate existing roads and the river, plus the retaining walls needed to reduce the area of land taken. The largest structure was the slender arch bridge which is now such a feature of the Memorial Park. This is actually two separate bridges, one carrying each carriageway.

Many local men worked on the project and one, Tim Martin, remembered it as his first job, as he was taken on as a "chain boy", assisting the site engineers in setting out the works, at a rate of 2s 9d (equivalent to 14p) per hour.

This was a world without application forms and formal interviews and, after spending ten weeks at Hicks Gate working on the roundabout and dual carriageway to the nursery, Tim secured a transfer to the workshop in pursuit of his ambition to be a plant mechanic. All the plant was owned by the contractor, so everything had to be repaired on site. This led to plenty of overtime and a full shift on Saturdays. It was good experience, although his duties included walking the mad dog that guarded the well-equipped workshop, and Tim stayed with the company for many years.

The new road was opened by Paul Dean, the Member of Parliament for North Somerset, on 27 July 1966. It proved something of a lifeline for the town two years later when it provided the only bridge over the River Chew after the flood of 10 July 1968.

1965
KEYNSHAM TOWN HALL COMPLETED

The first part of the redevelopment of Bath Hill and Temple Street to be completed was the two ranks of shops, which opened in 1961. Work on the Keynsham Town Hall progressed much more slowly. In October 1963 erection of the steel frame of the main block was underway and by the middle of the following year the shape of the building was clear and the frame of the landmark clock tower was in place.

Construction underway in June 1964

The new offices provided accommodation for the staff of Keynsham Urban District Council, together with a Council Chamber. Twenty-seven years after the idea was first mooted the "Civic Centre Opening Ceremony" was held on 1 October 1965. A reception and lunch was held at Saltford Hall and the guests of honour were Major Sir Egbert and Lady Cadbury. Former members of the Council and members of Keynsham Round Table were invited as well as civic dignitaries. After lunch, the party moved to the Civic Centre where the ceremony was held; this was followed by an inspection of the new buildings.

The completed Town Hall in late 1965

It had always been intended that the Civic Centre would combine a range of public buildings, with the Town Hall as the centrepiece; Somerset County Council were partners and a new County Library was one of the facilities. The County's presence was marked by the figure of the Somerset dragon, with its mace, mounted on a tall post. (This survived the eventual demolition and in 2020 was housed in the B&NES archaeology store.)

The new library replaced the one in the former Liberal Club premises on Bath Hill. This building had been used by the UDC for council meetings and by the Home Guard during the war; in 1941 it was decided to establish a public library there, but it is not certain when this was first opened. The UDC purchased it in 1944 and, as a library, the adults' section was upstairs and the children's downstairs.

In front of the Town Hall was a modest plaza, which rarely saw anything in the way of the public activities that the architect probably envisaged. However, it did provide an outdoor exhibition space for the Saltford Painting

The Library entrance in later years

The former Library building on Bath Hill, which had many short-lived uses after closure in 1965

Members of the Saltford Painting Club set up their Summer Exhibition in the 1970s

The Old Fire Station, replaced in 1965. In 2020, Card Factory occupied this site.

Club's Summer Exhibition during the 1970s and 1980s.

Part of the development, but of necessity a separate building, was the Fire Station, belonging to Somerset Fire Brigade, and also completed in 1965. It replaced the original station, a former coach house, at 65 High Street, which had served the town since 1928. With its hose-drying tower, yard and proper accommodation for the retained firemen, as well as bays for two appliances, the new station was a great improvement. It was used for exactly fifty years, becoming redundant on 18 October 2015 when the new Fire Station at Hicks Gate was opened.

When the Town Hall was being built, in 1964, a "Time Capsule" was buried in the base. This comprised a copper box containing coins and stamps, black and white photographs, copies of local newspapers and other memorabilia from the time. Little did those involved imagine that the block would be demolished and the box uncovered in less than fifty years' time.

1966
BLACKSMITH BOB TROTT RETIRES

The last blacksmith to work in Keynsham was Bob Trott; his smithy was at the top of Woodbine Steps, by the New Inn, in the building since converted into the skittle alley. He was a well-liked and jovial man and was always happy to have an audience whilst he was working; children used to stand in awe of him as he worked the bellows under his arm whilst heating the iron bars to the correct temperature. Short in stature, with a large paunch behind the leather apron he always wore, he was a real craftsman.

As a farrier, he shod horses of many different breeds, including the local cart-horses. The owners would bring their horses to the smithy, which had a distinctive smell of burnt hoof whilst he was shoeing them. In his other role as a blacksmith, Mr Trott was skilled at creating ornamental wrought ironwork for gates and fences to suit the buyer's requirements; he also made and fitted the steel rims for cart-wheels.

After a serious heart operation he had to give up the strenuous work, so he closed the business in 1966 and the town lost the presence of one its best-known personalities.

Robert Jellico Trott was born in 1915 to William and Edith, nee Williams, who came from Keynsham. His middle name was after Admiral Sir John Jellicoe, whilst his twin brother was named Edward Kitchener. Bob and his wife Ellen were married in 1940 and lived in Chew Cottages near the bottom of Dapps Hill. After he closed the smithy, he took on a light job at Fry's but lived only another two years before he died on 5 April 1968, at the early age of 52. He is buried in Keynsham Cemetery.

| 7 MARCH | The last passenger train ran on the former Midland Railway line from Mangotsfield to Bath. |

1967
DEMOLITION OF BRICK TOWN

Historically, Keynsham was a village built of stone. The local blue lias is a form of limestone, easy to quarry and suitable for building. Before the mid-nineteenth century, only one or two buildings, notably the Wine Bar (formerly the London Inn and Royal Oak), on the High Street, used other materials.

However, in 1879 a local builder constructed two ranks of houses as what would today be called buy-to-let properties on the land sloping down to the River Chew behind the New Inn. These comprised eleven small cottages on Woodbine Steps, running down towards the Chew, and a row of seventeen called Fairfield Terrace overlooking the river. They were built as cheaply as possible, with few amenities and were constructed of brick, rather than the local stone. Hence the development became known as Brick Town. When new, the water supply was from wells and even into the twentieth century, they had neither gas nor electricity – lighting was by paraffin lamp. In 1894, the local Medical Officer reported that some of the houses were unfit for habitation and in a storm the following year part of the brickwork of several was blown away. Improvements were made, probably reluctantly, by the landlords over the years but the properties remained of a poor standard.

In April 1967, the Council issued a Clearance Order and all the houses, along with the nearby Fairfield Gospel Hall – by now empty – were demolished the same year, with the land being added to the extension to the park.

The backs of the houses in Fairfield Terrace, shortly before demolition in 1967

The VE Day party at Fairfield Terrace, May 1945

1968
THE GREAT FLOOD

R arely does Keynsham or its locality make national news, but 11 July 1968 was an exception. The storm that swept across southern England the previous day and night was at its worst over the Chew Valley. It was followed by the most devastating river flood since the Lynmouth disaster of 1952, with loss of life and extensive damage to property and communication links across the area. For those who lived through it, the experience was one they will never forget.

Much has been written about the disaster, so we have researched the archives, found new accounts and with the perspective that the passage of time brings, looked again at the events and the legacy of the Great Flood of 1968.

I - THE STORM AND FLOOD

On Wednesday 10 July 1968, rainfall across a swathe of southern England from Dartmoor to The Wash broke all records, with several areas exceeding 4" (100mm) in 24 hours, whilst over west Mendip, Bristol and Kingswood the total was more than 5" (125mm). But the highest figure was in the upper Chew Valley, with 6.8" (175mm) recorded at Chew Stoke.

In Keynsham the rain started about mid-day, but from about 6.45pm it became torrential and continuous, punctuated by frequent thunder and lightning, until after midnight. The River Chew rose steadily and some of those with

gardens on the banks moved objects that might be washed away to safety. This intensity of rain was far beyond the capacity of the rivers and drains and during the night every brook, stream and river in the area burst its banks, causing devastation on a scale greater than any in living memory.

Roads became impassable; not just those that were low-lying, but many others where the flow of water from fields and gardens simply had nowhere else to go. Driving was difficult and for many motorists there was no route home that night, so they stayed with friends, relatives or slept at work.

The River Chew rose far above its normal flood levels. As it swirled through the upstream villages and farmland, well out of its banks, the surging water picked up branches, tree trunks, livestock, fencing and assorted debris. Bridges collapsed and about midnight a wall of water reached Keynsham; the surge first hit the Dapps Hill and Chew Bridge area, flooding some houses to above first-floor level and forcing residents upstairs. Minutes later it reached the Bath Hill Bridge.

The shops at the bottom of Fox & Hounds Lane were engulfed, trapping the occupants in the flats above. At about this time, a car carrying four people stopped on the bridge, unable to get through. The occupants got out, the two women tried to reach safety and the men pushed the car, but the force of the water swept them against the parapet. None could hold on and all were washed into the torrent. Only the young man, Charles Kaye, survived by grabbing hold of a tree; his parents and fiancée Alexandra Giles were drowned.

Further downstream the flood destroyed the footbridge leading to Keynsham Station and the arch bridge carrying Avon Mill Lane. The ancient County Bridge across the Avon also succumbed, leaving just a gas main as a precarious link. The final tally of material damage in Keynsham was three road bridges destroyed and one damaged, 24 houses and small shops substantially damaged, with a further 177 affected to a lesser degree. Seventeen families comprising 48 people had to be evacuated.

2 - WHY DID IT HAPPEN?

Very heavy rain leads to flooding, but why was the 1968 flood so severe and why did the main rush of water hit Keynsham so suddenly and with such force? It is worth trying to answer these questions.

Early July saw several periods of rain and catchment of the River Chew was well-soaked by the tenth. On that day an area of low pressure, centred on the Bay of Biscay, generated a band of heavy rain and thunderstorms along a line from the Bristol Channel north-eastwards to The Wash. The resulting rainfall totals were quite exceptional.

During summer storms, vegetation absorbs a surprising amount of water, in roots, leaves and on the surfaces. Next, the rain will soak into the soil if it can but, when the vegetation and ground are saturated, all the extra water begins to flow on top of the soil. This happens at about the same time right across the affected area, so although the rain may be falling steadily, at some point there is a sudden increase in the water on the ground. The soil then acts just like a tarmac road: a sheet of water covers the

Debris in Avon Mill Lane on 11 July

surface and flows down the slope. This "sheet run-off" occurred right across the Chew Valley on the early evening of 10 July.

The valley sides are generally fairly steep and the riverbed falls quite rapidly down to Pensford, Woollard and the other villages. So, the run-off reached the watercourses very quickly, and once there these were flowing fast. Water levels rose rapidly forming a surge that moved downstream: this was a classic "flash flood", a phenomenon that can be predicted but one that often takes downstream communities by surprise.

As the water in the river increases, other natural effects come into play. Looking at any river tells us that, in a flood, it flows much faster than usual. Normally, the water is slowed down by the friction of the bed and banks, but as flows increase it runs more freely and faster. As it speeds up, the water stores more energy, so its ability to carry trees, boulders and debris and to damage riverbanks and buildings increases enormously. This was shown by the debris left behind in Keynsham Memorial Park.

All eyewitnesses agreed that between midnight and 1am, a "wall of water" hit the Dapps Hill area and carried on downstream to the Bath Road Bridge. What caused this?

It was widely rumoured after the event that sluices at Chew Valley Lake had been opened. In fact, the lake was well below its capacity before the storm. During the night its level rose by 1'-6" (0.45m) which was remarkable, but left it well below the overflow. It has been calculated that had the dam not existed the volume of water flowing down the valley would have been up to three times as much, so the damage downstream would have been far, far worse. The small reservoir at Chew Magna did overtop during the evening, but this meant that it no longer reduced the flow in the river – it did not add to the flood.

The old stone bridges along the Chew Valley, with their small openings, formed barriers to the flood water; arches soon became blocked with trees and other debris, causing the water to back up until the pressure became too much and they collapsed, adding more material to be swept along. As each bridge gave way there would have been a sudden surge in the water

The Sluice-gate Wall at Chewton Mill

level and it has been suggested that there was a cumulative effect as successive bridges failed, leading to a bigger and bigger wave. This may have occurred upstream, but the valley varies in width, with some lengths such as between Compton Dando and Chewton Keynsham being quite wide, so such a wave would have diminished. But before Keynsham, there was a wall across the valley at the sluice-gates by Chewton Place. When this collapsed, the water had only half a mile to go to reach Albert Mill, where the valley narrows sharply, so the surge would have been deepened as it funnelled through. This could have created the "wall of water" that had such an impact.

3 - WORK BY THE FRY'S FIRE BRIGADE

Somerdale had its own fire brigade, with a core of sixteen men who lived in Chandos Road, plus auxiliaries; all had regular jobs at Fry's but took on fire duties when required. The Brigade had an arrangement with the County Fire Brigade to assist when possible during an emergency. In 1968, the Chief Fire Officer was Des Ryan, who wrote this account of his men's work during the Flood.

"..... *by 6.15pm the roads were awash and running like rivers. The bells [in our houses] rang and we were called out to pump out the flooded lift-wells along Hams Road at the factory - eight in all. We set pumps in A, B, C, D and O-Blocks and gradually lowered the levels so that the lifts could be put back into operation. We got back to the fire station about 9pm only to be told that the office basement was flooded to a depth of about four feet and still rising, so we set three pumps in; it was nearly midnight before we had succeeded in lowering the level to an acceptable couple of inches.*

"*We then received a message from Somerset Fire HQ to say that they were putting us on stand-by because the whole area was under threat and river levels were rising at an alarming rate. Meanwhile, I sent a couple of patrolmen down to the fields to*

The Works Fire Engine, purchased three years before the Flood

open gates so that the cattle could be moved to higher ground and for Mr Clapp, the farmer, to be notified of the danger. It was obvious that the Power House basement would soon be affected if the river continued to rise, so we set in pumps in readiness and had to start pumping about 3am.

"Before that though, a call from Somerset HQ requested our assistance at Dapps Hill, where people were trapped in their bedrooms. I could only spare one crew, who picked up a couple of canoes from the youth club, and on arrival, managed to paddle to the cottages to reassure the occupants that the flood level was falling and tell them that they would be safer in their bedrooms rather than risk being capsized out of a canoe!

"On returning to Somerdale, the crew informed me that the main roads were impassable and Keynsham's fire engine was trapped in ten feet of water at the Bath Hill Bridge, while hundreds of motorists were stranded in and around the town. So I asked the Catering Department to open up the kitchen and provide hot soup, bread and mugs of tea for any motorists and their passengers who wished to take advantage of it, after I had told the police that such facilities were laid on. A steady stream of motorists came on to the site and were very grateful for the refreshments. We were glad to be able to stop for a few minutes break and to change into some dry clothes too.

"It had been a terrible night. All the firemen were concerned about their families, so I stood down most of them at 6am and managed to get home about 8.45am. After a quick bath I was soon in the land of nod. When I awoke, I noticed that the flood water had reached our garden wall and Mr Clapp and his son were swimming in the sports field trying to round up the remnants of their cattle, taking them to the higher ground adjacent to our house.

"Back at work, I had more requests for assistance at Saltford and Dapps Hill. I sent a crew with canoes to Saltford to ferry supplies of bread and milk to the households that were cut off along Mead Lane and gave Keynsham fire station hoses, standpipes, hard brooms and so on, so their men

could hose down the roads and pavements in the Dapps Hill area. We had a request from Keynsham UDC to clean and dry carpets from flooded homes; so we fixed up wooden beams across the roof trusses in the laundry and hung the carpets up to dry after hosing the mud and slime off out in the road. This job seemed to be never-ending and in the end I wondered if people were deliberately messing up their carpets just so they could get a good scrub; I supposed it helped with claims for insurance companies as well!"

4 - RECOVERY

Daylight on Thursday 11 July revealed a scene of devastation around the Chew and Bath Hill Bridges. The water level was still high but falling, revealing mud, twisted railings, broken walls and masonry, tangled tree branches and half-submerged cars in the lower part of the Memorial Park; the shops at the bottom of Bath Hill were badly damaged, their contents strewn around.

Recovery work began immediately with public authorities and volunteer groups involved. By mid-morning a relief centre for the homeless had been set up at Broadlands School along with a rest centre at Queens Road Methodist Church. Each centre received over twenty people from flooded properties, who were provided with dry clothing, food and drink

Bath Hill Bridge became unsafe and was closed

whilst alternative accommodation was being arranged.

Next, the cleaning up began. Once again, volunteers came to the fore in assisting Council staff with such jobs as clearing away debris and the thick coat of mud and slime left everywhere, and in disinfecting affected properties. They also cleaned and prepared vacant Council-owned cottages scheduled for demolition, so they could be used by displaced families. The sewage pumping station in the Memorial Park was out of action so cleaning and replacing the electric motors was a high priority.

Local firms also gave support, directly or by releasing staff to help in the clear-up. Geoff Mabbs' breakdown truck winched several cars from the river while the office of the Keynsham Chronicle acted as a furniture mart and information/advice centre.

The main Bath Hill Bridge was badly damaged and had lost most of its parapets. It was open only to pedestrians but after lunch a hole opened up in the road surface as more of the arch below collapsed. It was clearly unsafe, so the bridge was closed completely, leaving the by-pass providing the only link across the river.

It was a top priority to reinstate the principal road links and the Army came to the rescue with a scale and speed of response that was remarkable. Having installed a bridge on the A37 at Pensford on the Saturday, 125 soldiers moved to Keynsham and immediately started work at Bath Hill on a 150ft (46m) long two-lane girder bridge, which was opened to traffic on Tuesday 16 July. Replacing the County Bridge across the Avon followed but this was a more difficult job, carried out by another unit and completed about 29 July. The bridge on Avon Mill Lane, giving access to the Brass Mill area, did not justify the expense of a temporary bridge so this road had to remain closed until a permanent replacement was constructed.

5 - RECONSTRUCTION

Over the following two years the temporary bridges were replaced. Bath Hill Bridge was rebuilt on a new alignment and at a higher level, requiring demolition of the row of shops that had been so badly flooded. The three arches were replaced by a single span to give space for a much bigger river flow than before.

At the County Bridge there was a similar improvement and the opportunity was taken to straighten the road; the course of the Avon was also changed, so it is now hard to imagine the original layout. In fact, it had long been an aspiration of the highway engineers to make these improvements but the two county authorities had never agreed on a scheme: the flood made the decision for them.

On Avon Mill Lane, a replacement bridge was built, again slightly higher than the original.

Refurbishing the damaged homes took longer, but most people were able to move back

May 1970. Concrete beams for the new Bath Hill Bridge were brought by rail to the Goods Yard and then transported by lorry.

October 1970. The new County Bridge approaches completion behind the Bailey Bridge, which is on the line of the old road.

during the six months after the flood. One or two were unable to get over the horrors of that night and never returned; for many others the experience took a long time to recover from.

At Dapps Hill, the ancient little bridge had survived, with just the loss of its masonry parapets, so today the wrought iron replacements give the sharp-eyed observer a clue to the event in 1968.

Two years before the flood the opening of the Keynsham by-pass saw the construction of a new high-level bridge over the Chew. The river channel through the park was realigned, reprofiled and lined with stone. When the flood came none of these new works caused any obstruction to the flow, though the channel was completely submerged by the volume of water, so no improvements were necessary.

6 - THE LEGACY AND LESSONS LEARNED

A disaster on the scale of the flood leads to upheaval and change. At a personal level there was bereavement for two families, enormous stress and anguish for many more. Over time, the mental scars heal but in many cases they never disappear entirely. To have one's home flooded is a horrible experience. The physical fabric can be repaired but treasured possessions will be lost and, worse, the victim is often left with a sense of insecurity that can last many years, sometimes for ever. Even when it is irrational, the sound of heavy rain can revive memories and cause anxiety. One of those rescued as a child from Gooseberry Lane says that if she has a bad dream it always involves water, boats and drowning.

At another level the consequences of a disaster are beneficial. There is a natural response, by both individuals and organizations, to say "this must never happen again" and to make changes to try and ensure this. After the flood, changes and improvements were extensive.

The Bristol Avon River Authority had the responsibility for managing the River Chew; they had a duty to ensure the free flow of water along it and to regulate the activities of the landowners along the banks so they did not interfere with the river. There was no requirement, nor at that time any general expectation, that they would provide a system of flood warning. Ten years before the flood, the authority installed flow gauges on the rivers, including one at Compton Dando on the Chew. Technology did not then enable remote reading of the water levels but this was introduced later (in 2020 they can be checked by anyone via the internet). These gauges then enabled staff to check the river levels constantly and by combining these with readings from local

Flow-measuring station at Compton Dando

rain gauges to predict increases and hence imminent flooding. A system of flood warning was thus developed, although the steepness of the Chew Valley means that there can never be much notice of precise water levels.

In addition, the Authority embarked on a major construction programme of flood alleviation schemes (the words "flood prevention" were never used, as it is impossible to guard against every conceivable flood) across their area. This was to take many years and was continued after the River Authority was abolished in 1974 and subsumed into the Wessex Water Authority. Neither organization had the powers to raise the funds required and all schemes had to be approved by the Ministry of Agriculture, Fisheries and Food to obtain grant funding, which could be a lengthy process. On the River Chew, river improvements were justified only in the Chew Magna area, with none around Keynsham.

It is routine for all the authorities involved in an emergency operation of this kind to review their response and to examine how they could do better next time. Since 1996, river management has been the responsibility of the Environment Agency and they work with other organizations to minimize and manage flood risks.

In 2008, the agency produced a booklet about the 1968 flood entitled "Learning the Lessons". The greater part of this was devoted to descriptions and accounts of the flood and its aftermath on the several villages upstream of Keynsham. It also described the work of the Agency in keeping river channels clear and how its modern flood warning service operates; alongside this is a section on what the Agency terms Flood

Resilience, which gives practical advice to riverside residents on how to prepare and stay safe should another major flood occur.

This resilience approach is a recognition that although the rain that fell on 10 July 1968 was quite exceptional, it would be neither realistic nor affordable to enlarge the river channels to deal with such enormous flows of water. The new bridges would not obstruct the water as the old ones did but the reality is that if such rain occurred again, widespread flooding and severe damage would be inevitable.

7 - MEDIA COVERAGE

The exceptional storm passed across much of southern England and caused severe flooding in many places, so it was not only the Chew Valley and Bristol that made the national headlines in print and broadcast media.

Locally, though, the disaster dominated the news for several days. Produced in Bath, the Keynsham Weekly Chronicle devoted its front page for Saturday 13 July to the story, along with four pages of pictures inside. Before then, the Keynsham edition of the New Observer, part of the Bristol Evening Post Group, had speedily produced a special edition on Thursday containing an eight-page picture supplement: 35,000 extra copies were printed.

The editor of the Bristol Evening Post gained a head start in realising the severity of the disaster as, returning from an event in Peasedown St John, he spent the evening of 10 July stranded in a pub near Keynsham from where he arranged by phone to produce an additional four pages for Thursday's edition.

Despite the collapse of normal telephone and communication services the paper included six pages of news and pictures on the floods as well as the four-page picture supplement. Further supplements followed on the next two days and the Evening Post sold 64,000 extra copies over the three days.

Despite the extensive newspaper coverage at the time there was little in the way of a comprehensive account of the flood and its immediate aftermath. As the twentieth anniversary approached, this prompted Terry Staples, who lived in Keynsham, to rectify the omission before it was too late; he researched and compiled a collection of reports, accounts and pictures which he published as *"The Great Flood of 1968"*. Most accounts written since draw on his valuable research.

8 - COMMEMORATING THE FLOOD

For those who lived here at the time, the flood is probably the most memorable local event since the end of Second World War, so it is not surprising that the anniversaries in 1998 and 2018 were remembered in music and performance events, most notably in a musical called *"Bridge Across the Flood"* in which many people participated.

However, no physical memorial had ever been erected so, as the fiftieth anniversary approached, the Local History Society decided to realise a proposal made years before: to re-erect the "County Bridge Stone" that had, for centuries, marked the boundary between Somerset and Gloucestershire on the bridge over the River Avon that was destroyed in the flood. The stone, probably originally from Keynsham Abbey but conceivably Roman, had been recovered from the river and was in the care of the Council's archaeology team. With the co-operation of the Parks Department, substantial support from Keynsham Town Council and donations from individuals and businesses, a scheme was designed and funded to place the stone, together with a commemorative plaque, in the Memorial Park.

Notwithstanding a last-minute scramble to get the work completed on time, a ceremony was arranged for the day of the anniversary, 10 July 2018, and in hot sunshine the plaque was unveiled by Cllr Karen Walker, the Chair of Bath and North East Somerset Council.

1969
BONZO DOG BAND LP

Keynsham has an interesting link with 1960s group the Bonzo Dog Band. The group originally formed in 1962 as the Bonzo Dog Doo-Dah Band and successfully combined comedy with a variety of musical styles, including jazz and rock. They had a couple of name adjustments before eventually shortening it to the Bonzo Dog Band in 1968. By then the growing fanbase already called them the Bonzos.

The key members of the band included Neil Innes and Vivian Stanshall, who wrote the majority of the Bonzos' material. They came to fame appearing in The Beatles' *Magical Mystery Tour* film at the end of 1967. Around this time they were also hired as the resident band on *Do Not Adjust Your Set*, an afternoon children's television comedy show, notable for starring several future members of Monty Python (Eric Idle, Terry Jones and Michael Palin), Denise Coffey and David Jason in the cast. The band performed every week as well as sometimes participating in sketches.

In 1969, the Bonzos issued their fourth LP with the title *"Keynsham"*. The title track was written by Neil Innes as homage to Horace Batchelor, whose adverts on Radio Luxembourg in the early 1960s were part of the teenage years of many post-war baby boomers. Horace Batchelor's voice can be heard at the start of the album's first track *"You done my Brain in"*. The Bonzo Dog Band is now remembered in Keynsham in the name of one of the café-bars in the new civic centre and their LP cover is one of the images on the clock tower.

The Keynsham album is a continuation of the Bonzos' interest in Horace Batchelor. The group's first album *Gorilla*, released in 1967, when they were known as the Bonzo Dog Doo-Dah Band, contains a track called *The Intro and the Outro*. This Viv Stanshall song starts by introducing the members of the band and their instruments and then namechecks a long list of random characters playing an increasingly unlikely range of musical equipment. Horace Batchelor, Harold Wilson and Adolf Hitler are three of those mentioned.

JULY	The Keynsham and District Horticultural and Industrial Society, founded in 1887, held its last meeting.

1970
THE LAMB AND LARK

GEORGES BRISTOL BEERS

PROP. H.A. PENNEY.   TEL. 31. KEYNSHAM.

In the medieval period, alehouses were ordinary dwellings where the householder served home-brewed beer; inns, by contrast, were purpose-built to accommodate travellers, and taverns sold wine. Each of these advertised their businesses with a sign hanging outside or, in the case of ale houses, a pole garlanded with foliage. From the fourteenth century, inns and taverns hung out a pictorial sign by which they could be identified in the then illiterate age. The term Public House came into use in the eighteenth century.

Keynsham has always been well-furnished with public houses although many have disappeared over the years. In 1841, there is evidence of nineteen public houses, alehouses and inns in the town and it was said that Keynsham had so many pubs it was impossible to have a drink in them all and still remain standing!

There have been two Lamb and Lark Inns in Keynsham. The first was on the junction of the High Street and Bath Hill leading down to Back Lane. It caused a sharp bend which was declared to be too dangerous for horses and carts so the Inn was closed and sold. Meanwhile a new Lamb and Lark was established on the High Street and opened on 21 March 1745 by William Thomas, the licensee, who was also an excise officer with his office on the premises. For many years inquests were held here, the most famous leading to the trial of a ten-year-old boy found guilty of causing the death of a young lad by pushing him into the River Avon.

Brian Vowles, a local historian, was born and bred in Keynsham on Bath Hill and the Lamb and Lark played a great part in his life for many reasons. For example: during the Dunkirk evacuation of 1940, Brian's father went missing for a few days but on arrival back in England he

49

was able to phone the Lamb and Lark, the only local place which had a phone, and a message was passed to assure his wife that he had returned safe and sound.

After the war, Brian's parents both worked in the hotel and at the Palm Court Ballroom which was at the rear of the Lamb and Lark. Weekly dances there were very popular, attracting many people from Bath and Bristol looking for a good night out. Music was provided by Charles, a blind organist. Brian remembers well that on Sunday mornings it was his job to hose the nicotine off the potted palms!

As well as dances, many dinners such as for the volunteer militia in the 1890s, wedding receptions and other social activities took place there so that the Lamb and Lark became a focal point of the town. Various bodies such as the Board of Guardians of the Workhouse had used it for meetings and Brian's great uncle Jack Exon held practices for the Town Band on the premises in the 1920s and the 1930s. At one time, the yard was even home to the town's fire appliance.

Over the years, as the town grew in size and the Fear Institute and Drill Hall offered new venues, the popularity of the Lamb and Lark gradually faded; during the 1960s it went into decline and was eventually closed. To the regret of many it was demolished on a Sunday morning early in the 1970s, to be replaced by a supermarket, leaving only memories of this long-established meeting place.

5 JANUARY	Saltford Station closed.
SEPTEMBER	A Son et Lumiere comprising fourteen episodes was performed to commemorate 700 years since the founding of St John's Parish Church.

1971
THE SHIP INN REPRIEVED

The Ship as it was in November 1971

This pub lies near the south end of Temple Street and is one of the oldest in Keynsham, with the building dating back to the late seventeenth century or, if the date on the iron fire-grate is to be believed, 1636; it has stone mullion windows as used from the later date. It may not have been built as a public house but has been one for several centuries; the bar names use old naval terms such as foc's'le. When it was built, the bridge at Dapps Hill may well have been the only bridge over the Chew, making Temple Street the road to Bath. The section of the building on the left was originally a stable.

The planned redevelopment of Temple Street in early 1970s envisaged the demolition of every building along the east side of the road. Local people fought to retain the two pubs included: the London Inn and the Ship. In the end the London Inn was lost, although the landlord took the name with him when he moved to The Royal Oak on the High Street. The Ship, however, was of greater historic interest so in November 1971 it was given Grade 2 listed status, enabling it to escape the wrecker's ball.

As landlords and customers' tastes have changed the building and its uses have altered. The former snug has been opened out and the rear garden was the base for a successful petanque team in recent years.

---

3 JULY   The Key Youth Centre, behind Keynsham Victoria Methodist Church, opened.

1972
ASHTON WAY CONSTRUCTED

In the centre of Keynsham the basic layout of the main streets remained the same for several hundred years, with the Parish Church at the junction at one end of the High Street, and Bath Hill falling away from the start of Temple Street at the other. Rock Road was constructed in the early 1900s and the bottom of Charlton Road was greatly widened before the present buildings were constructed about 1966.

Behind the buildings lining the west side of the High Street were long gardens, some of them narrow, and areas of orchard. The map on the right dates from 1902 and shows these clearly.

In the 1960s, car ownership increased rapidly; Keynsham High Street was the main road from Bristol to Bath until 1966. Despite the by-pass, traffic congestion became steadily worse and there were no off-street car parks of any size. Eventually, the Council approved a radical plan: to construct a new road along the rear of the High Street, giving access for unloading at the back of shops, together with a large public car park. This meant the demolition of buildings in Charlton Road above the Victoria Methodist Church, and near the bottom of Rock Road, with various outbuildings. The western edge of this expanse of tarmac was defined by the old footpath, which still survives, known in the twentieth century as Scouts' Way.

Construction underway in April 1972

Following the necessary land acquisition, which involved numerous landowners, clearance began in 1971 and construction of the road and the first section of the car park the following year. The car park was extended a few years later. The road, and hence the car park, was named Ashton Way in tribute to Mr George Ashton, the long-serving former Clerk to Keynsham UDC.

1973
TOM CARPENTER, HAULIER

In 1973, the last member of the Carpenter's Haulage business, Tom Carpenter, died. The firm had been a permanent fixture in Keynsham life for two centuries, providing a vital service to residents and businesses alike. It is hard to imagine nowadays how people transported goods and sometimes complete households before the advent of the combustion engine but the answer is – by horse and cart. The company is first listed in Kelly's Somerset Directory in 1906 with the proprietor shown as Mrs Anne Carpenter, unusual in itself; the stables, for several shire horses, were situated on a smallholding adjacent to the Recreation Field (now the site of The Hawthorns). Recreation Lane was renamed Carpenter's Lane when the area was redeveloped.

Tom Carpenter often delivered heavy loads of logs to the logwood mill - Albert Mill - in Dapps Hill, which meant tough work for him and his horses as they struggled down the steep hill, but no serious accidents were ever reported. The stone bollards at the side of the road are believed to have been used to wedge the wagon wheels to slow and control the descent and to give the horses a rest when climbing the hill. Tom also had the contract to roll the town's cricket pitch – then situated on the Recreation Field – which he did after fitting his horses with soft overshoes so as to avoid damaging the 'square'.

There was a steady decline in the number of horses used for haulage between the wars but they were not uncommon in 1945. We have no illustration of Tom Carpenter's horses but the picture, taken on the site of the Fry's factory in 1922, gives a flavour of the work.

On 1 January 1948, Tom lost his business when much of the road haulage industry was nationalized. By this time, he had eight lorries but still had a few working horses. His lorries became part of the British Road Services fleet, but Tom could see no future in the large organization and left the industry – Carpenter's Haulage had reached the end of the road.

2 AUGUST	As part of the Bristol 600 celebrations, a horse-drawn mail coach passed through Keynsham and Saltford, complete with coachmen and passengers in period dress.

1974
KEYNSHAM BECOMES PART OF WANSDYKE AND AVON

Local government organization and council boundaries are not subjects that set the pulse racing. However, the changes made to local government on 1 April 1974 were so far-reaching that no history of the period can ignore them.

The county of Somerset was created by the Normans in the eleventh century. The name appears to have first been used in the eighth century when the area was part of the Kingdom of Wessex. Somerset County Council was created in 1889, along with other county councils and county boroughs across England and Wales. It was responsible for the major administrative functions of local government such as education and highways.

At a lower level, services in this area were provided by Keynsham Urban District Council, which came into being in 1938, when Keynsham and Saltford were taken out of the area of Bathavon Rural District Council. These local councils had responsibilities mainly related to public health and welfare and included refuse collection, sanitary services, sewerage, housing, street-lighting, cemeteries, libraries, parks, controls on buildings such as petrol stations, and licensing of public entertainments.

In 1972, central government decided that these arrangements, with a large number of very small authorities – such as Keynsham UDC – were outdated and inefficient. They were to be replaced by a new two-tier structure with new counties around major centres of population. Bristol was such a centre and Avon was created around it. Somerset survived but it lost its northern part to the new county.

Below the new county council were the six district councils shown on the map. Keynsham

THE COUNTY OF AVON WITH DISTRICT COUNCILS

KEY :
1. Wansdyke
2. Bath
3. Bristol
4. Kingswood
5. Woodspring
6. Northavon

and Saltford were in the new District of Wansdyke. Named after the sixth-century earthwork that ran from Dundry, around the south of Keynsham and across to Englishcombe, this was a somewhat artificial area, with two main centres of population: Keynsham and Midsomer Norton / Radstock. Apart from being in the same county, these two centres had little in common and have never been connected by main road or railway, so the new council had something of an inbuilt tension when it came to deciding where resources should go.

As far as Keynsham and Saltford were concerned, the changes meant that local matters were being decided by councillors from a wider area; the loss of autonomy was keenly felt and on the last day of its existence the UDC held a Civic Service at St John's to mark its passing.

In fact, the new arrangements had only a short life. Local politicians in Bristol, and Bath

Procession to the Civic Service on 31 March 1974, the last day of existence of Keynsham UDC

as well, never really accepted the County of Avon, although there was logic in centralizing some functions, so both Avon and Wansdyke were abolished on 31 March 1996. Local government services in Keynsham and Saltford were then handed to a new single tier authority – Bath & North East Somerset Council – which moved its principal offices to the new Civic Centre in Keynsham in 2015.

Before long, it became apparent that there really were benefits in co-ordination between the local authorities across the greater Bristol region in some activities, such as strategic planning and transport, and this led to the setting up of the West of England Combined Authority in February 2017.

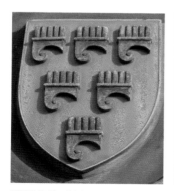

KUDC Shield, based on the Arms of Keynsham Abbey

Wansdyke DC Shield

4 AUGUST   Keynsham Police Station ceased opening to the public 24 hours a day.

1975
KEYNSHAM LIVESTOCK MARKET CLOSES

T here is evidence that the market began before the turn of the nineteenth century, just off the Bath Road. In 1887 *"The Gazetteer of the British Isles"* states there was a market-day in Keynsham on Thursdays; at the time the town's population was 2,482. The site is believed to have been the area behind the row of terraced houses at the bottom of Chandag Road. However, as business grew, access to the site became too difficult and dangerous for vehicles so it moved to the other side of the main road, on the land adjacent to the Talbot Inn, where the McCarthy & Stone homes now stand. The site was almost an acre in size and operated on Mondays until it closed in 1975.

As dairy farming was the predominant practice in the area, many barren dairy cows and calves were sold through the market, but also a good entry of beef cattle, sheep and pigs satisfied the requirements of not only the local butchers but also regular buyers from Bristol and Bath. The Gazetteer also states that sheep and stock fairs were held twice a year, in spring

and autumn, when breeding cattle and sheep were sold.

During the early and mid-twentieth century there had been a large number of butchers in Keynsham, including Pearsalls (the only one still trading in 2019, now as The Wright Butcher's), Frays, (formerly Connetts), Woodruffs (formerly Brownseys), Shears, Olds, Rawlings, Gill and Down; at least three of these had their own slaughter-houses in the town, so they bought livestock direct.

The very last market on 31 December 1975 was conducted by Mr David Elder, senior auctioneer for Cooper and Tanner, who had the sad task of ringing the hand bell summoning buyers to the sale for the last time. However, the very last animal sale was by Mr Harold Dowdney who was a local JP and a retired director of Cooper and Tanner. In 1923, he had moved from Glastonbury to Keynsham to take over the practice of Albert Ford, later re-named Cooper and Tanner, a task he carried out successfully for over fifty years; it was felt appropriate that he should have the honour of bringing down the hammer for the last time.

In 1975 the lease of the land on which the market stood ran out and it was eventually sold. Efforts were made for the market to continue by joining forces with the auctioneers at Bridgeyate, but these failed, so local farmers had to take their animals to the markets still operating at that time: at Winford, Frome, or Chippenham.

| JUNE | Keynsham Chamber of Commerce proposed that the High Street be made traffic-free. |

1976
RIVERSIDE OFFICES OCCUPIED

The Temple Street Riverside office buildings, completed in 1975, are reputed to have been originally planned as a hotel in the first phase of the Chew Park Development. However, the site never fulfilled that function and the buildings were occupied in 1976 by the South West Region of the British Gas Corporation, the nationalized body which ran the gas industry. Each region had its own management structure and around 400 workers moved to Keynsham from various premises in Bath.

It was a four-storey building above the ground floor reception and shops, in two wings (north and south) with an interlinking building/corridor. As the headquarters, it contained six directorates, as well as a directors' suite and subsidised staff canteen.

In 1986, British Gas was privatized, using the "Tell Sid" advertising campaign to sell shares to the public, and giving British Gas South West a regional monopoly of gas distribution and supply. They also owned showrooms, but appliances were increasingly available at competitive prices from other retail outlets.

Ten years later, the regional monopolies were broken up, their functions passing to Centrica, known as British Gas, and Transco. This was soon followed by the opening up of retail gas supply to competition. Restructuring meant that staff numbers had been falling gradually, so the large headquarters was no longer required; some staff moved whilst others went to other jobs, retired or took redundancy. Bath & North East Somerset Council then rented part of the building for office use.

The building was completely out-of-scale with its surroundings, visually overwhelming the Temple Street area. It was vacated by B&NES Council when they moved to the Civic Centre in 2015 and then was unused, except for parts of the ground floor. Various proposals were considered before the Council acquired the lease and redeveloped the blocks through a development subsidiary to provide 95 flats. Changes included giving the blocks a lighter colouring. In December 2019 the first occupants moved in.

| JUNE TO AUGUST | In the summer of 1976 England experienced the worst drought of the century with Chew Valley Reservoir so low that the remains of old buildings could be seen. Temperatures were above 30°C for several weeks. |

1976
LEISURE CENTRE OPENS

The Swimming Pool immediately after opening in 1976

Plans for a swimming pool in Keynsham were first considered by the Council in 1951. At that time, there had been no new pools built since the war and most that existed were in larger towns and cities. Forecasts showed that a substantial subsidy would be needed to run a pool and in the economic climate of the time this could not justified. Times changed, the population grew, and Keynsham Leisure Centre, incorporating much more than a swimming pool, was opened by Councillor Doug Miles, Chairman of Wansdyke District Council, in March 1976.

Prior to this, Keynsham residents had to travel several miles to a swimming pool, the nearest being the Jubilee Baths in Knowle. Wellsway School pupils were bussed to Broadweir Baths in central Bristol.

The original Chew Park Development plan, conceived by the then Urban District Council in 1971, was for the development of Temple Street from the current Fire Station to Dapps Hill. It generated great local opposition because it included demolition of many houses as well as the Ship Inn and the London Inn. After much consultation, planning permission was finally granted by Somerset County Council's Planning Committee in June 1973 for a reduced scheme allowing the reprieve of the two pubs. The first phase would be flats, followed by the second phase comprising a leisure centre, offices, shops and a restaurant.

The leisure centre was behind shops in Temple Street, with access by lift or down a flight of stairs. A sports hall catered for badminton, table tennis, trampolining and gymnastics. Various fitness and dancing classes were run. There were two squash courts, a sauna and a 25-metre swimming pool with viewing gallery backed by a tea and coffee bar – later replaced by coin-operated machines. The Olympic Bar, overlooking the swimming pool, was later converted to a gym/fitness area.

During the first year, there were several developments and problems. Early on, Sunday morning swimming for disabled was introduced – later becoming Keynsham Seals – and an application was made for a licence for special occasions. At the same time, there were reports of vandalism, disputes regarding bookings and concerns about running costs. Public Health Inspectors demanded essential work on sinks and hot water supply estimated to cost £40,000. By December, Wansdyke Council's Finance Sub-committee was recommending that charges would have to be raised and staff cut or reorganised.

The problems were overcome and since then, daily swimming pool timetables have enabled a wide range of users to enjoy it at different times: Scouts' session (until the 1990s), early morning and lunchtime swimmers, schools, under-fives with adults, swimming for fitness, adults only, over 50s and learners of all ages. The pool became home to Keynsham Amateur Swimming Club, which helps young swimmers to progress from the Preliminary Squad to the Masters Squad. It is the venue for regular competitive swimming galas and Keynsham's junior schools compete at an annual swimming gala.

Of the other activities at the Leisure Centre, badminton has always been popular and there are well-established groups meeting at different times of the week; some of these have been running for many years.

Management of the Leisure Centre changed after 2004 when the Council contracted out the operation of its leisure facilities to Aquaterra for a ten-year period. In July 2015, the next contract was awarded to GLL, a charitable social enterprise, which trades under the name of Better.

After about forty years, increasing running costs and the need for major repairs meant the future of the Leisure Centre, and the swimming pool in particular, was reviewed by Bath & North East Somerset Council in 2015. Various alternative sites were considered for a replacement but, after public consultation showed that many users wanted the facility to remain on the same site, a phased programme of rebuilding and improvement was started in 2017 at an eventual cost of about £11m. The first phase, including an improved fitness suite and a soft play area, opened in June 2019 and the whole scheme, with the rebuilt swimming pool and a new teaching pool, was due for completion in spring 2020.

| MARCH | Whiting's Furniture Shop in Keynsham closed after 280 years as a family business. |
| JULY | Dutch Elm Disease gradually swept the countryside. Planners forecast that 70% of elm trees in the Avon Valley would be lost, but eventually all died. |

1977
TWINNING WITH LIBOURNE

Visitors from Keynsham take a trip on a traditional gabarre in 2015

After the Second World War, town twinning became popular, as an act of peace and reconciliation; a way of fostering friendship and understanding between different cultures and former foes. Bristol was twinned with Bordeaux in 1947. After a series of reciprocal visits between local councillors, a twinning charter was signed by officials of Libourne, near Bordeaux, and Wansdyke District Council in 1977.

Both Keynsham and Libourne have rivers running through them and farmland on the outskirts, although Libourne's main form of agriculture is grapes and wine! Keynsham's ancient Abbey is in ruins but Libourne still has many buildings dating back to the Middle Ages.

Out of the charter grew:

- School exchanges between pupils from secondary schools in Keynsham, Norton Radstock and their counterparts in the Libourne area. These continued until the 1980s.
- The formation of Wansdyke Twinning

Keynsham ✕ *Libourne*
Keynsham & District Twinning Association

The twinning website features an image of Keynsham merging seamlessly into the River Garonne

Association to lend administrative support. The name changed to Bath & North East Somerset Twinning Association, and later to Keynsham & District Twinning Association to reflect the catchment area of members.

- Reciprocal exchange visits, inspired by friendships developed between teachers involved in school exchanges.
- Annual educational visits to Keynsham by wine students from Collège de La Montagne near Libourne.
- Introduction of corporate membership, with exchanges between Keynsham Orchestra and Libourne Choral, the involvement of Somerset Morris in several exchanges and teams and groups such as Keynsham Rugby Club and Wansdyke Judo.
- Youth involvement with work placements in Keynsham for Libourne school leavers and a visit to Libourne by members of Keynsham Youth Council in 2014.
- A programme of social events.
- The setting up of a website.

A core part of the twinning arrangement has been exchange visits between adults, travelling at their own expense and being hosted in homes. These group visits take place regularly and include trips to places of interest,

Somerset Morris dancing in the Market Place, Libourne 2015

communal meals, social events, and time for friends to spend together.

Between visits, members in Keynsham have enjoyed regular social events such as Bastille Day suppers, quiz evenings and coffee mornings. Such events promote awareness of the group as well as raising funds for local charities and to entertain visitors.

2017 saw the fortieth anniversary of the twinning charter and a visit to Keynsham by the Libourne Mayor and Councillors. To mark the occasion, the Libourne Lounge in the Civic Centre was dedicated and plaques were unveiled, followed by a special celebratory lunch.

7 JUNE	The Silver Jubilee of the Queen's accession to the throne was marked by 12,000 street parties across the country including many in Keynsham and Saltford.
8 AUGUST	As part of her Silver Jubilee programme of visits, the Queen came to Keynsham.

1979
CYCLE PATH TO SALTFORD

The 1970s was a period when environmental concerns were of great importance to many, as the generation born after the Second World War grew up determined to make the world a better place. This desire took many forms and on College Green in Bristol in 1977 a meeting was held of cyclists who were worried about the dominance of the car in political thinking and planning. Out of this meeting grew the 'Cyclebag' campaign group, later to be renamed 'Sustrans'.

Led by a dynamic young civil engineer, John Grimshaw, the group determined to do something practical to improve the lot of cyclists and show that there was an alternative to building only new roads. Their first project was to convert the former Midland Railway line from Bristol to Bath into a cycle path.

Matters of land ownership and complications from existing roads and structures meant that the length from the edge of Bath to Bitton was the first part to be tackled. During the summer of 1979 five miles of usable pathway, two metres wide with a stone dust surface, were completed along this stretch, which passed through Saltford. The work was undertaken by a small army of volunteers, often up to fifty strong – including children – who spent their weekends camping and working. At the end of the summer the track was officially opened with a ceremony that included the Minister of Transport.

At this point the path from Saltford was merely a local link, and it took until 1986 to complete the route through to Bristol, but it proved popular from the start and showed that there was a need for such paths. Sustrans developed a plan to extend the concept and by the mid-1990s they had built cycle paths all over the country, mostly along old railway lines, but these were not linked together. In 1996, the Millennium Commission backed Sustrans by awarding the first Millennium Grant of £42million, to develop the National Cycle Network, which led to a network of routes, both on and off-road, totalling 5,000 miles, being completed by the year 2000.

As part of this National Cycle Network, the Bristol to Bath Railway Path now forms a short stretch of Route 4, which is continuously signposted, though not all off-road, for the 432 miles from Greenwich to Fishguard.

1982
ROGER NUTBEEM – FALKLANDS WAR

When the Falkland Islands were occupied by Argentine forces in April 1982, the British Government dispatched a task force to recover them. The ensuing conflict cost the lives of 255 British military personnel, one of whom was Major Roger Nutbeem from Keynsham.

Roger was born at Redditch in April 1942 and after attending Alcester Grammar School he went on to agricultural college, followed by two years in Holland working and studying Dutch dairy farming. He then changed direction and joined the Royal Army Medical Corps aged twenty, qualifying as a dispenser. His potential was soon recognized and he was selected for officer training in 1967, then commissioned into his old Corps - the RAMC.

After training RAMC recruits, Roger was posted to the RAMC College as 'house officer'; whilst there Roger developed his adventure training skills, becoming an expert canoeist and mountain expedition leader. In addition, he was a keen folk singer, playing a somewhat battered guitar that went with him on exercises and became a welcome feature of team entertainment during long deployments. His knowledge of dairy farming proved useful on exercise in Germany when his unit was camping in a barn. One of the cows was struggling in labour; Roger sorted her out and delivered the calf, using a block and tackle! When the farmer arrived, he was a bit concerned to see all this going on without him, but it was soon schnapps all round.

Roger was totally committed to the RAMC, and had an ability to motivate people. He was never happier than when working with young people who shared his enthusiasm and zest for life. In Keynsham, he spent three years as second in command of the 219 (Wessex) Field Hospital, based at Ashmead Road. Later, he was appointed to 16 Field Ambulance RAMC which was deployed to the South Atlantic as part of 5 Brigade. He sailed south in Queen Elizabeth 2, continuing to chivvy, cajole, challenge and generally inspire his men on the voyage.

After visiting Ajax Bay when he landed on 2 June, Roger travelled round to Fitzroy in the RFA Sir Galahad on 8 June. The ship was attacked there by Argentine fighter-bombers, and Roger was killed instantly on the upper deck by a bomb fragment. His body was later recovered to shore, temporarily interred, and then repatriated to the UK. He now lies in the military cemetery at Tidworth.

Roger left a widow, Tricia, whom he had married in 1970, and who was appointed MBE for the work that she did for the 16 Field Ambulance Wives Club in the aftermath of the Galahad disaster. They had two children: Martin and Kathryn. Tricia and the children returned to Keynsham and made it their family home.

1983
KEYNSHAM TALKING NEWSPAPER

A recording session in progress in 2017

In April 1983, Mary Burnard gathered together a group of ten people to discuss the possibility of producing a Talking Newspaper for blind and partially-sighted people in and around Keynsham. It was found that there was a potential of about a hundred residents in the area who could benefit from a service of this nature, so it was agreed to run a trial for a period of six weeks.

Two groups were formed: one of these prepared thirty minutes of local news items and the other worked to produce content for a similar period, concentrating on magazine material. This proved to be a very successful format and so the first tapes were circulated on 10 June 1983 to eighteen homes. They were enthusiastically received and over the years the number of listeners grew steadily. By 2001 there were 240 registered listeners including not only local residents but people living in Belfast, Cumbria, Cornwall and Surrey who had links with Keynsham, although the number has fallen significantly in recent years.

There are some 500 Talking Newspapers in the UK and, in 1991, Keynsham Talking Newspaper was proud to win the National Competition as the best of its kind in the country.

The service is completely free and all the work of running it is done by volunteers, with about seventy involved in total. Roles include the readers who find their own material, the editorial team and the technicians who manage the recording of the master tapes and the copying of them. Behind the production work is a committee, which concentrates on raising funds and buying the necessary equipment.

Like any newspaper, it runs to a strict timetable, with the reading and recording on a Thursday and dispatch by the post team via the Post Office on Friday. Special yellow wallets are used, and Royal Mail delivers them without charge. Originally, the content was recorded on tape, which was then copied. Technology has advanced and the advent of digital recording means that listeners are now provided with play-back machines for use with a USB memory stick.

1987
PASCOE'S DOG FOOD

Rick Pascoe was born in 1918 into a poor Cornish family and died in 1988. He and his wife Roma had three children: Tony, John and Tessa. After living in a council house in Selworthy Close in Keynsham, they moved to the Tunnel House at Saltford. For most of his life, Rick worked for Sainsbury's Agricultural Merchants in Trowbridge; then, in 1980, he started a business with his wife and son Tony in a barn in the grounds of Manor House, Nunney. They manufactured cattle and calf food under the name F A R M (Flaked Animal Ration Manufacturers).

A proud mother with her hungry litter

Later, he saw an opportunity to make a complete dog food. The name was changed to Pascoe's Ltd in 1987 and the manufacturing process moved to Broadmead Lane in Keynsham. The food consisted of wheat, maize, barley and peas which were steam rolled, cooled and dried on jog trays to give a flaked mixture. To this were added pellets (dried meat, fish meal, protein concentrate, minerals), making it a pioneer health food for dogs. It was bagged by hand and grew to be a UK market leader, selling two hundred tons per week.

This was a high-quality product with an old-fashioned image. The packaging, designed in the 1980s, reflected this and some took the product to go back to the 1890s. Later, Pascoe's Dog Food was sold to Sheldon Jones of Wells, and it later became Pascoe's PLC. The Keynsham factory closed in 1989 and the business was finally bought out by C & D Foods, who still manufacture the Pascoe's brand in East Yorkshire.

During his life, Rick was Commodore of

A customer helps out in the factory yard

Saltford Sailing Club, President of Keynsham Lions Club, started the Keynsham Gymkhana (held in the triangular field at the junction of Durley Hill and Old Bristol Road, known as Rick's Field) and hosted Conservative Club functions.

1988
JOHN PASCOE'S ROYAL OPERA DEBUT

I n 1988, Saltford-born John Pascoe made his debut at the Royal Opera House, Covent Garden as director of a production of "*Anna Bolena*" starring Joan Sutherland. He lived with his family (his father Rick founded the dog food company) in Tunnel House, Saltford and his first venture into theatre design was in 1968 when he designed the Fry's panto production of "*Babes in the Wood*". He initially earned his living by teaching art at Prior Park School in Bath but the lure of the professional stage proved too much.

His debut as scenery designer came in 1979 when he designed for Handel's "*Guilio Cesare*" for the English National Opera and won the *Evening Standard* Award. He subsequently worked as director/designer for such opera houses as Chicago, San Francisco, Dallas, Houston, Spoleto Festivals USA and Italy, Rome, Cannes, Munich, the Royal Opera House and Sydney Opera House. He has created new productions, mostly of the bel canto and baroque periods, featuring the greatest names of the operatic world. Five have starred Dame Joan Sutherland, and six Renée Fleming.

Since 2000, John has worked closely with the great Spanish tenor Placido Domingo and was described by him as "an excellent collaborator".

John in a wig from Don Giovanni

His work as director and designer has been consistently praised for its intelligence, style and fidelity to both the music score and the text. His career spans forty years and shows no signs of slowing down, with projects planned in major opera houses across the world.

John's love affair with opera started in early childhood listening to recordings of Mario Lanzo and Dame Joan Sutherland and, in later life, he became a lifelong friend and Dame Joan's favourite director.

JANUARY	The Fry Club presented its last pantomime, "*Robinson Crusoe*", at the Fry Hall before the venue closed permanently.
I OCTOBER	Local girl Nicola Shear represented Great Britain at Seoul Olympics in the final of the synchronised swimming event, finishing seventh.

1993
MANOR ROAD COMMUNITY WOODLAND

We often think of history as accounts of events, people and buildings, but in the last thirty years work in the countryside between Saltford and Keynsham has added another dimension to our local history. Several fields totalling over 50 acres (21 hectares) have been converted from agricultural land to form a recognized Local Nature Reserve as part of the Forest of Avon.

Each compartment of the woodland has retained its original field name, based on the tithe map of 1840. These are known as Middle Tyning, Hurn, Poor Hurn, Moor Close, Breaches and Plaishets. Hurn is an old English word meaning corner of land or land in an angle, tyning is an enclosure, and the word plaishets implies marshy ground.

With the help of many people including pupils at Wellsway and Chandag Junior Schools, planting commenced in 1993; another field was added in 2001. Over 19,000 trees and shrubs have been planted and are now slowly beginning to mature. A large open meadow, a haven for butterflies and other insects that feed on the flowers, can be found and a natural pond is home to frogs, toads, newts and dragonflies. It has become a favoured spot for dog walkers as well as local naturalists.

Primroses are abundant from late February and cowslips in April. Field scabious and musk mallow thrive throughout the summer. Butterflies include marbled white, silver-washed fritillary and numerous meadow browns. Hawfinches spent parts of 2009 and 2018 in the woodland and up to 160 waxwings visited in 2005. Bat and tawny owl boxes have been installed to help with diversification within the woodland.

The site is owned by Bath & North East Somerset Council who maintain the woodland

Early morning sun reaches the pond on a cold morning

May blossom by one of the paths

with help from a Friends Group set up for the purpose. The lead mentor was Nigel Jacks until his premature death in 2015; he was presented with a Town Council Good Citizen Award for his work there. For several years, Keynsham Town Council has awarded the group a grant to help with the management. The reserve has been widely recognized as a good example of a community woodland, winning several awards and featuring in the BBC's *Autumnwatch* on television and Radio 4's *Shared Earth*.

1994
KEYNSHAM MUSIC FESTIVAL

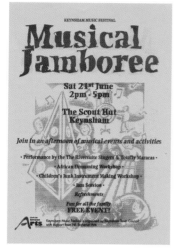

1997 Event Flyer

1998 Event Flyer

2002 Programme

It is uncertain which year the Keynsham Music Festival began! The programme for 1997 welcomes visitors to the Fourth Keynsham Music Festival, so the assumption is that the first festival was held in 1994. This was organised and funded by Keynsham Town Council with the support of North East Somerset Arts. It is likely that, in the first few years, the festival took place on one afternoon in the summer.

By 1997, the scope of the festival had become more ambitious with events running from 21 to 29 June. A Musical Jamboree took place on the afternoon of Saturday 21 in the Scout Hut – a free event, fun for all the family. There were performances by The Riversuite Singers, Totally Maracas and an African drumming workshop. Various events throughout the following week were held at venues around the town including St John's Church and Wellsway School. Keynsham Brass Band played in the park on Sunday afternoon.

It is thought that following the 1997 festival, the Keynsham Music Festival Association was formed from the Keynsham Town Council Music Festival Committee. In 1998, on Sunday 19 July, a Musical Funday was held in the Memorial Park for the first time. To mark the thirtieth anniversary of the 1968 flood, over 150 local people took part in "A Bridge Across the Flood" – commemorating the flood through music and songs at Wellsway School on 18 July. This was the first festival organised by the Music Festival Association in the current form. As such it can be viewed as the first Keynsham Music Festival. The 2003 programme welcomes visitors to the Sixth Keynsham Music Festival.

In 2000, the country singer Fred Wedlock, best known for his hit single "The Oldest Swinger In Town" performed at the festival. Attendances continued to grow and in 2001, the local paper reported that the total exceeded 10,000. That year, and in 2002, The Wurzels – the Scrumpy and Western band from Somerset – performed on the main stage to great acclaim.

By 2003, the format which endures to this

2018 - Ellis Grover walks the tightrope to show the depth of flood water in 1968

day had emerged with four separate stages in the Memorial Park and workshop tents providing adults and children with opportunities to take part. The performance stage had performances by a number of local organisations including children from the Keyford Dancing School.

For the past twenty years, the Music Festival has grown organically, attracting more visitors year on year. It has remained free, funded by grants from The Arts Council, Bath & North East Somerset Council and sponsorship from local firms. As the festival grew in size, the costs and logistics of staging the events grew. In 2012, The Keynsham Music Festival Association became a limited company. The festival remains fully supported by Keynsham Town Council and four town councillors are on the board of Trustees. In 2016 the Association achieved charitable status.

Year on year the festival grows in popularity. During the week of the festival, many artists and bands play in venues around the town. On Saturday night, the Keynsham Orchestra play Proms in the Park with the second half of the programme mirroring the last night of the proms in the Royal Albert Hall. The Committee aims to introduce something new each year and in 2018 staged the first ever opera in Keynsham, with a performance of "La Bohème". That year also saw a re-enactment of the 1998 "A Bridge Across the Flood" performance, with some added drama provided by a high-wire performer demonstrating the flood level in the park!

Almost all the planning is done by volunteers and the Festival Committee spend many hours during the winter selecting the bands to play at the next event, from the hundreds of demo CDs they are sent. In 2019 the cost of staging the festival was in the region of £90,000 and although Sunday has by far the biggest programme – and pulls in the crowds – more events are now being staged on the preceding days. Although its origins may now be a little hazy, in 2020 The Keynsham Music Festival is an established part of the town's life, enjoyed by many.

Matt Bond of Stevie and the Masquerades

1995
SALTFORD BRASS MILL RESTORED

Saltford Brass Mill is a unique remnant of an industry that dominated industrial life in the Avon Valley in the eighteenth century. The site was recorded in the Domesday Book as a corn mill and in later centuries the mill was used for fulling, the thickening of woollen cloth, until the late 1600s. In 1702 Abraham Darby started making brass at Baptist Mills on the River Frome in Bristol and about twenty years later this work was transferred to Keynsham's Avon Mill, because of its better water supply. The brass ingots were then transported up the river to this mill at Saltford and others at Kelston and Weston. At Saltford and the other sites the earliest main process involved the shaping of brass sheets into hollow-ware vessels such as pans, bowls and vats.

Originally, large water-powered hammers were used to beat the brass ingots into sheet and then faster hammers shaped the sheets into the hollow-ware. The beating process was known as battery and hence Saltford was known as a brass battery mill. Technology progressed and rolling mills (pairs of heavy rolls working like an old-fashioned mangle) were soon introduced to roll the ingots, as they produced more even sheets. Hammers continued to be used to shape the sheets into hollow-ware.

Although the brass was malleable enough to be worked cold, it began to crack after a certain time. To prevent this, the partially worked brass was periodically softened by heating or "annealing" it. A large furnace was soon developed locally so that the brass goods were protected from damaging fumes. The remaining Saltford furnace, once one of four at the mill, is the best surviving example of this important innovation.

Manufacturing at Saltford reached a peak in the early 1800s and declined thereafter,

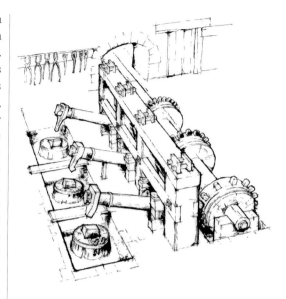

An impression showing how the hammers may have looked

although Saltford villagers had to wait until 1908 for closure of its last noisy brass hammer – which by then was probably the last of its kind in western Europe. The brass rollers continued working until 1925, when the site closed altogether.

Parts of the site and buildings then had other uses – including conversion to a squash court – but by the 1970s the brass mill was derelict and demolition was becoming a real threat.

That the mill survives as a building and as a museum is due to the efforts of Joan Day, who devoted much of her life to studying the industrial archaeology of the area and, in particular, the local brass industry. She realised that the ruined buildings were in danger of being lost and started an energetic campaign to save and restore them to provide future generations with an opportunity to learn about this unique aspect of local life.

The Brass Mill in 2019

The first objective was to have the surviving buildings "listed" and after assessment by English Heritage this was achieved in 1975, with designation as Grade 2* because of its special historic interest. Next, the Bristol Industrial Archaeological Society surveyed the mill and, in 1981, the site was leased by the Avon Industrial Buildings Trust. After further work the site was further Scheduled as an Ancient Monument in 1986.

Whilst the buildings were now legally protected, it proved difficult to develop a means of raising sufficient funds to restore them without altering them so much that their special character would be lost. A public inquiry into one such proposal in 1986 rejected changes on these grounds; English Heritage then commissioned further archaeological investigations. These led to English Heritage fully funding conservation works at a cost of £170,000, provided that a new trust was established to manage the site and that there would be future public access to the mill. They also required a commitment regarding future maintenance, and to ensure this the lease was taken over by Wansdyke District Council.

With these commitments in place major structural conservation took place in 1995. Since then work by the local authority and the Brass Mill Project volunteers have ensured the future of this fascinating industrial relic.

1 APRIL	Keynsham Paper Mill, built in 1933 by E S & A Robinson, was closed by its then owner, Sappi.

1999
KEYNSHAM DANCE CENTRE CLOSES

A carnival float in the 1970s - the girls wear wellies to protect their dancing shoes

In 1964, journalist Rodney Vince, who ran the Keynsham office of the Bath Evening Chronicle, decided on a change of career. Having trained with Lionel Kibble of the Imperial Ballroom, Bedminster, he decided to open a dance school in Keynsham with his wife, Joan. Initially the school was called the Satin Slipper School of Dancing and, for the first two years, they ran classes in ballroom and Latin American at various halls around Keynsham including the Co-op Hall and Saltford Hall. In this time they built the school from a handful of pupils to over 200.

The dance school found a permanent home after the Urban District Council moved to the new Town Hall and sold the premises they owned at 9 Wellsway, Keynsham in 1966. Vince and Joan, who lived at 7 Wellsway, obtained the lease for the temporary building at the back from the new owner. This became the Keynsham Dance Centre and provided a permanent home for the school for the next 28 years.

In 1969, Rodney contracted meningitis and was unable to teach for three months. Joan ran the school single-handed with the help of parents and friends. She learnt to drive and took to the road in a yellow Reliant Robin.

In the 1970s, disco fever came to Keynsham with the Dance Centre running disco classes

Joan's retirement with past and present pupils, 31 March 1999

for adults and children in the British Legion Hall. The Dance Centre played a full part in the life of Keynsham, with a carnival float, dance performances at fêtes and tea dances. Over the life of the school, pupils took over 10,000 awards during a total of 135 examination days. They won 80 gold cups and several former pupils now run dance schools themselves.

Rodney Vince died in 1982, aged 53, and Joan continued running the school. In 1994 the lease on the studio at 9 Wellsway expired. Joan reluctantly concluded that she could not afford the terms of the new lease and so went back to running the classes at various halls around Keynsham. Without a permanent home, running the school was more difficult. Eventually Joan decided that she could no longer continue

and hoped to find someone to take over from her. Unfortunately this did not happen. Joan retired on 31 March 1999 and the Keynsham Dance Centre closed. As a final irony, and by sheer coincidence, the studio at 9 Wellsway, which had been home from 1966 to 1994, was demolished the same day.

Disco in the studio in the 1970s

2000
CANNOCK'S GARAGE CLOSES

Cannock's Garage with Homeleigh Cottage behind, probably taken in the early 1960s

Cannock's Garage stood at 36 Bristol Road, Keynsham from 1919, when Mr Edward Cannock Senior opened it, until 2000 when it was closed.

Behind the garage, a little hidden, was a cottage believed to have been built in 1685. This was one of Keynsham's most historic buildings and in 1975, when it was not in a good shape, it was declared a Grade 2 listed building; in 1990 it was noted as being of special architectural historic interest. Gradually, it fell into a very poor state of repair, and eventually English Heritage declared it as being beyond any sensible restoration. Originally the cottage was at road level, with a garden and two apple trees at the front, but successive road improvements left it noticeably lower than the neighbouring buildings.

Edward Arthur came to Keynsham in 1910 travelling in a 'Trimo', a ten year-old three-wheeler made locally by the Avon Motor Company. He was looked after by an aunt at No 36, once known as Holmleigh Cottage, and married a young Keynsham lady, Elsie Taylor. In June 1923, Edward John was born followed by Betty in 1924 and David in 1933. After David's birth the family moved to 14 St Ladoc Road and No 36 became a store and office for the garage.

Keynsham Urban District Council granted a licence for a petrol installation in 1926 and in 1928 the garage became a Morris agency. Two years later, electric pumps were installed and were believed to be the first to appear on the Bristol to Bath Road. In 1938 the main workshop was extended rearwards and a new fascia was installed; the building was of reconstituted Bath stone, as Edward wanted something permanent. The forecourt was concreted and the apple trees removed.

During the Second World War, Mr Cannock arranged for No 36 to become the headquarters of the ARP (Air Raid Precaution) Heavy Rescue Group with a 20hp Austin breakdown lorry with crane made available as a support vehicle – this was used during the Bath Blitz. The back room of the garage was reinforced with steel girders to form a strong shelter. Edward and the Clerk to the Council (George Ashton) were appointed joint officers in charge of the ARP Report Centre based at the court building adjacent to the police station on Bath Hill.

Throughout the war the garage maintained the UDC vehicles although there was a certain amount of 'make do and mend' due to a shortage of spare parts. Part of the main workshop was portioned off to form a machine-shop. Ministry of Aircraft Production authority was granted to produce aircraft components for Bristol Aeroplane Company. Five to seven men were engaged in making blank gauges to be finished at the Horstmann Gear Company in Bath, and between 1941 and 1945 about a quarter of a million items were made.

Post-war, the machine-shop was utilised to make sundry engineering products as well as items for the garage trade, needed as cars laid up during the war were brought back into use. Morris and Ford agencies were retained for supplies of new cars, which were very limited; waiting lists for customers were up to a year.

During the 1950s there was little machine work but in the lower showroom a new brick frontage with teak and glass doors was built. A contract was awarded to Cannock's by Somerset County Council to maintain and house vehicles for the School Meals Service based at Broadlands School. Before long, there were changes in petrol brands; pressure from National Benzole to move to a single brand for a six-month trial was resisted and the garage continued to sell Shell. As car production increased over the years it became impractical to do justice to two major marques so the Ford agency was given up, whilst that for selling Morris vehicles was kept.

Edward Arthur Cannock, apart from running the garage with his sons, was very much involved with the life of Keynsham, being Chairman of the Urban District Council for some years and representing the town on numerous committees.

Eventually, the garage was closed with the retirement of Edward John and David Cannock. The old cottages collapsed in 2001 and the site was redeveloped for housing.

Re-boring work in the machine-shop, 1940s

A Cannock's advertisement from 1962

29 APRIL 2001   The national population census was held and recorded the population of Keynsham as 15,533 and that of Saltford as 4,153.

2005
CHARLTON CINEMA DEMOLISHED

Keynsham Town Band played at the opening on 7 September 1936

Keynsham's first cinema was on the High Street. This operated from 1908 to 1914 and although a success at first, it became unprofitable and closed, the building being sold at auction to become a garage, later the St Keyna Motor Works, and eventually in 2010 the site of Coffee 1. However, in the years following the end of the First World War, the popularity of the silver screen continued to grow and there was a demand for a cinema in Keynsham.

After several years of proposals, objections and problems, building of a new cinema on Charlton Road began early in 1935: the art deco-style Charlton Cinema was opened in 1936 by Miss Gwendoline Wills, of the tobacco family and a prominent local social worker, in her capacity as Chairman of Keynsham Picture House Ltd. On the opening night long queues formed and every one of the 879 seats, including 330 on the balcony, was soon occupied.

Patrons were escorted to their seats by usherettes who sold ice-creams at the interval. At that time cigarette smoking in public buildings was normal and people recall that it was sometimes difficult to see the usherettes through the blue haze. The more expensive back row seats were a favourite place for courting couples, although wily customers in cheaper seats at the front often found ways to move there.

"Picture-going" became one of the main forms of popular entertainment and people travelled for miles in all weathers to watch a programme consisting of a main and a supporting film, which changed twice a week.

Films were not the only attraction at the Charlton. With a stage twenty feet deep and four dressing rooms it was used for theatre performances and musical events. During the Second World War, it was a focal point for spreading public information through films, talks and meetings. In 1953 colour films of the Coronation and the Ascent

The Charlton Cinema in 1997

of Everest were shown. The 1960s saw queues down to the High Street to see the latest Beatles' films but, overall, audiences dwindled: the cinema was unable to compete with the popularity of television and videos, whilst cinemas in Bath and Bristol were showing films as soon as they were released. The Charlton finally closed as a cinema in 1984 with a showing of "*Terms of Endearment*".

Several attempts were made to use the site profitably as a bingo hall, but it never attracted sufficient custom, and the Charlton finally closed its doors in 1998. The building was put up for auction, failed to sell and became derelict and vandalized. Some efforts were made to prevent demolition, including a failed attempt to have it listed, but none of the various proposals were financially viable.

The building was finally demolished in 2005 and the site redeveloped by Oval Estates to provide a block of fourteen flats.

In the early years the cinema advertised by distributing small folding programme cards. A surviving example is shown:

2005
KEYNSHAM FILM WORKS

The demise of the Charlton Cinema meant that film-lovers in Keynsham had no local venue to visit and this lasted from 1984 to 2005. In that year, Keynsham Film Works came about thanks to the enthusiasm and energy of Suzi Mizrahi, who at the time was the Town Council Arts Development Officer, and a group of local Keynsham enthusiasts. A committee of eight was elected and it was decided to show films on the first Thursday of the month from September to May, opening doors at 7.15pm for a 7.45pm start.

It was decided to run the venture as a club and the subscription in the first year was £25: sixty-three members were enrolled. Membership has stayed fairly constant but the numbers attending are usually between fifty and eighty as many people, who are not members, simply turn up on the night, and pay for admission. For the most popular showings such as *"Testament of Youth"* the audience has exceeded one hundred.

The committee, whose aim is to bring interesting films to a big screen in the heart of Keynsham, select a variety of films. Members are then invited to make suggestions which the committee then vote on until there is agreement on the final ten to be shown in a season. The first film ever shown was *"Before Sunrise"* starring Ethan Hawke. Last season, 2019-20, the planned programme ranged from *"Green Book"*, an account of a 1962 road trip across the American Deep South, through the factual *"Apollo 11"* to the Japanese *"Shoplifters"* and included films by Polish, Russian and German directors.

When Keynsham Film Works began screening the venue was the Fry's Club building. They then moved to Broadlands School and in 2015 moved again to The Space, part of the new Civic Centre complex, which offered an auditorium with high quality audio-visual equipment and, most importantly, raked seating. This has proved to be an excellent venue and in 2020 the group continues to flourish.

2006
KEYNSHAM HOSPITAL CLOSES

The Workhouse as it was in 1898

The last patients left Keynsham Hospital in August 2006, prior to its demolition to make way for a modern Health Centre. For many people, this building played a big part in their life in Keynsham, not only as a hospital but, earlier, in its role as the town's Workhouse. A summary of its history, with glimpses of life within its walls, is given below.

Keynsham Union Workhouse 1837-1948

As a consequence of the 1834 Poor Law Amendment Act, local parishes throughout England were required to make provision for the poor. In 1836, the newly-formed Keynsham Poor Law Union with its twenty-six strong board of elected local guardians was tasked with finding a suitable piece of land for the construction of a building that would provide a place of refuge for 300 destitute local persons. A three-acre site on land above Dapps Hill was located and purchased for the sum of £40.

In 1837 the Workhouse was built by local builders V and W James at a cost of £4,500. It was a rather austere building, with its traditional square construction, designed by William Armstrong, surrounded by 8ft high walls. Once inside you were stripped of your usual clothing; men were then issued with corduroy trousers and boots, while women were given long skirts and striped aprons. The living accommodation was separate for male and female, including married couples.

All the residents of the Workhouse were expected to work, including tramps and overnight stayers who were required to break down stones which would be sold on. This, along with the sale of oakum (the unpicking of old ropes by residents – 'money for old rope'), and the sale of garden produce would help to make the Workhouse self-sufficient. On a day-to-day basis the Workhouse was 'ruled' by an appointed Master and a Matron, along with a small number of staff including a cook.

At this time Keynsham had a population of approximately 2,400, with about a quarter listed as paupers. In addition, the Union also served the surrounding nineteen parishes with many more 'calling at the door' for food and overnight shelter. Following a wash, the overnight stayers would bed down on straw mattresses in the workhouse outbuildings. During the summer months of 1841, 1,486 persons were recorded as 'called at the door'; so the site was quickly becoming a very important community institution.

The 1881 National Census provides a detailed breakdown of the staff and 'inmates' resident at that time within the Keynsham Union Workhouse. Mr John Holt was the master in charge, with his wife Emily, who was the matron, (their ten-year old son was also resident) along

Some surviving outbuildings in 2020

with other staff members; a schoolmaster, a porter, a nurse and an Industrial Trainer of Girls. There were 117 residents in all with a wide age range from two months to 88 years, but each had something in common: they were all paupers. Some with a disability (under the heading of handicap) were listed as 'dumb' or 'imbecile'.

There was also a wide range of occupations listed, such as shoemaker, domestic servant, quarryman, hawker, general labourer, wheelwright, brick-layer and one man who was born in Sheffield, tin man. Twenty-five child residents under the age of fourteen were listed as scholars.

A closer examination of the census also reveals family relationships, with several unmarried mothers and their children, for example Jemima Willington, eighteen years, and her two-month old son Albert; both were born in the Workhouse. Once a person entered the Workhouse it was very difficult to find a way out of the social downward spiral; in particular, the elderly who, without any family support and no pension (the 1908 Pension Act made provision for men over 70 years), found times very hard and many died as paupers.

In 1890 the well-known local practitioner, Dr Charles Harrison, would also tend to inmates along with those at the nearby isolation hospital (also known as the 'Fever House') on the site of

what is now the Elim Church in Balmoral Road, for those suffering from the more contagious illnesses such as tuberculosis.

It was the responsibility of the Workhouse not only to record details of all inmates, but also by 1837 to register births, marriages and deaths for the parishes. The Master of the Workhouse took on the role of superintendent registrar.

In 1930 the Board of Guardians was abolished and responsibility for the Workhouse passed to Somerset County Council. The name was changed to Clements House, a name it kept until 1948. Throughout the Second World War the establishment continued to operate, providing accommodation mainly for children, single mothers and the elderly.

Keynsham Hospital 1948-2006

On 5 July 1948 Keynsham Hospital became part of the new National Health Service; in 1950 further legislation required the establishment to deal with sick persons only. This was brought about primarily to regulate the provision of medical care in the community but, in the case of Keynsham Hospital and many others, it helped to erase the stigma of the building being a place of residence for the poor and destitute.

The hospital became very much community-based with essential additional funding provided by local charities and the annual hospital garden fête, which from 1964 onwards was organised by the League of Friends. This fête became the focal point for the fund-raising and throughout the 1960s and 1970s was a major event in the town's social calendar. The funding helped to provide those extra treats for patients to enjoy.

In 1952 the hospital was recognized for the training of pupil nurses and soon started to provide a wider range of services, with a Physiotherapy Department for out-patients opening in 1956. By the 1980s Keynsham Hospital provided twenty beds for maternity cases, twelve beds for the physically disabled and fifty-four beds for geriatric patients, all within five wards. It incorporated a day-hospital taking up to eight patients with departments for Physiotherapy (including out-patient treatment) and Occupational Therapy. Staff were about 140 in number, consisting of 85 nurses, plus trainees, a nursing officer and a full-time sister in charge of each ward. Medical cover was provided by the local GPs and a Consultant Geriatrician.

Keynsham Hospital in 2006, shortly before closure

The rising costs of running a hospital in an old building designed originally as a workhouse, along with demands on the local health authority to restructure according to budgetary and care requirements led to a reduction in the services offered. In 1985, 113 babies were delivered at the hospital and many more mothers were admitted for postnatal care, but despite determined campaigns against the decisions, the maternity unit was closed in 1988 and the last patients left Keynsham Hospital in August 2006.

Keynsham Health Centre - Built 2008

Much of the Workhouse was demolished in 2007 to make way for the Keynsham Health Centre, although some of the original stone boundary walls and outbuildings remain in 2020. The new building was constructed by Kier Western at a cost of £7 million.

The Health Centre does not have any in-patient facilities. It provides accommodation for the Temple House General Practice, which serves 6,600 patients from Keynsham, Saltford and surrounding villages and employs five doctors. Also included are a dental surgery, accommodation for other NHS services and an adjacent pharmacy.

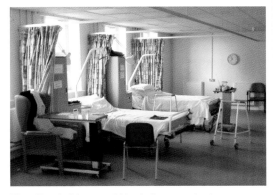

The Claude Harrison Ward, showing the last two male beds, before closure.

3 OCTOBER 2007   Cadbury announces proposals to close the Somerdale site by 2010.

2009
KEYNSHAM SCOUTS' CENTENARY

Keynsham Scout Group was formed in 1909, only two years after Lord Baden-Powell held his experimental camp on Brownsea Island that led to the founding of the Scout movement.

The Centenary was Saturday 7 November 2009 and a commemorative open day was held at the Scout HQ in Ashton Way, followed by a reunion and celebration evening. On display were items of memorabilia: pictures of Baden-Powell opening the West Country Jamboree at Corston in 1932, copies of Scout Gazettes, pictures of Beavers, Cubs, Scouts and Explorers through the years and uniforms of the 1960s and 1970s. Former members were able to try their hands at Scout skills demonstrated by young members.

At first, groups of boys met informally but soon acquired a Scoutmaster with a programme of camping, outdoor activities and training. Originally, the group met in an orchard off Bristol Road and then in the old school-house in Station Road before moving to the Lower Drill Hall in Bristol Road and finally to Ashton Way.

The growth and success of Keynsham Scouts in the last century was due to several outstanding leaders. The first was Vivian Turner, who moved to the town and took over as leader in 1928, having been a Scout leader in Bishopston. He provided the site for the group's first permanent headquarters and, despite being confined to a wheel-chair by polio, his energy and vision drove the group forward until his death in 1949. He built up a pattern of annual activities with camping at its centre, involving attendance at the Somerset Jamboree each Whitsun and a week's summer camp, usually in west Somerset or Devon. He left the whole of his property, including what

Vivian Turner

is now the Ashton Way car-park, to the group.

After a period of uncertainty, Tom Tookey emerged as the new leader of the group; his enthusiasm and love of practical skills gave many boys the pleasure of camping and many rewarding experiences.

By the early 1960s Keynsham was expanding rapidly and the group needed to grow, to run several units of scouts etc, or to change, by setting up several separate groups. At this time Ron Duggan, known as Dixie, appeared on the scene and under his visionary leadership the modern Keynsham 'super group' was created. He realized the value of the land they owned in the centre of the town and negotiated with Keynsham Urban District Council to sell part of it. The outcome was that the land on which part of Ashton Way car park was built was sold for £45,000.

The management committee had to decide what to do with this large windfall: plans were being made to build a replacement headquarters

1st Keynsham Scout Troop summer camp at Thorverton, Devon in 1957

building when the opportunity arose to purchase 30 acres of land near Chelwood, which had been offered to them to them at a discounted price, to use as a permanent campsite. It was decided that the chance to acquire the land at Chelwood was a unique opportunity – the building project could wait.

The land purchased was grazing land, on the edge of woodland. Tree-planting was needed and soon commenced, with Japanese larch and sessile oaks being planted during an early 'Father and Son Camp'. These have been added to over the years whilst other trees have been cleared for housekeeping reasons, with the wood used on site. Practical amenities were added between 1979 and 1982 with a water supply and a mobile toilet unit. In the early 1990s buildings comprising a barn and toilet block were constructed, making the site more usable, especially in poor weather. Chelwood became not only the home for the group's own camps and activities but also a source of income as it could be hired out to other groups of Scouts, Guides and other organizations.

At the time of writing, early 2020, 1st Keynsham Scouts continues to thrive as one of the country's most successful groups, providing practical and social experiences for over 300 young people aged between six and twenty-five.

28 AUGUST	Irene Rosenfeld, chairman of Kraft Foods Group, met Roger Carr, chairman of Cadbury's, to propose a takeover deal.

2011
SOMERDALE CLOSES – THE END OF AN ERA

To mark the end of production at Fry's Somerdale factory in 2011 we have written a brief history of the company and the site up to its redevelopment in 2014.

******

To a casual observer at the turn of the twentieth century, Keynsham Hams was a peaceful place, a rural setting of flat fertile farmland and grazing cattle, with the occasional game of football as Keynsham Football Club played a home fixture. This, however, was going to change in a major way when, in 1920, the land was surveyed as a site for a brand new chocolate factory. J S Fry and Sons were coming to Keynsham.

'SWEET BEGINNINGS'

The story of chocolate-making in Bristol dates back to 1729 when a patent was granted by King George the Second to Walter Churchman. His business was taken over in 1761 by Joseph Fry who had, up to that time, been an apothecary selling chocolate in Stall Street. Following the acquisition of the highly regarded Churchman's Patent Chocolate brand, business grew and by 1764 Joseph Fry had a network of over sixty agents selling his products all over the country. In 1847 Fry and Sons successfully developed a form of eating chocolate (as opposed to drinking chocolate) which, although coarse and rather bitter by today's standards, was extremely popular. Shaped into blocks and bars, and poured over fruit-flavoured centres, this chocolate was a real breakthrough, and in 1875 the Chocolate Cream bar went on sale, making it the world's first brand of chocolate bar.

In the second half of the nineteenth century, business expanded rapidly. Between 1860 and 1907, Fry's opened seven new factories in Bristol and by the time they became a registered private company in 1896 there were nearly 4,500 employees. However, J S Fry's faced fierce competition from other Quaker-based confectionery firms, namely Cadbury's, Rowntree's and Terry's and the First World War resulted in difficult trading conditions for all. In 1918, Fry's merged their financial interests with their main competitors, Cadbury Brothers Ltd and the British Cocoa and Chocolate Company was formed. The Fry family, believing that both firms were of equal value, were shocked when Cadbury's assets were found to be three times as much as theirs and consequently, when the shares in the new enterprise were allocated, Cadbury's held the controlling interest. Twenty-six-year-old Egbert (Bertie) Cadbury DFC joined the Fry's part of the collaboration following a falling out with his Quaker family

A foreman waits for the lift down, November 1922

1922 - The steel framework for A Block, seen from the excavation for the Power House

over his wartime service (he had been a fighter pilot) and, finding the premises in Union Street totally unsuitable for modern manufacturing processes, began with Cecil Fry to look for a suitable site outside Bristol to build a new state-of-the-art factory.

'EARLY DAYS'

The search ended with the selection in 1920, and subsequent purchase, of the land at Keynsham Hams, bounded by the River Avon – needed to provide cooling water – and the Great Western Railway main line from Bristol to Paddington. Railway access was needed so that workers could travel to the new factory with ease and, after the GWR gave permission for the creation of a spur line directly onto site, to bring raw materials in and finished goods out.

The first phase of development began in 1922 with the construction of two large, linked, longitudinal blocks of four and five storeys, several other four-storey manufacturing buildings and a large powerhouse. The main production blocks were constructed with steel frames encased in brickwork and concrete, making the buildings easier to alter at a later date to meet any future, more advanced or altered methods of manufacture. A Block was built first and limited production started in 1925; B Block was completed in 1928. During the works, evidence of Roman occupation came to light with the discovery of two stone coffins, containing the remains of a man and woman, the foundations of a villa and various artefacts, all of which were removed for safe

Company housing on Chandos Road was constructed in 1927

keeping. The villa foundations were reconstructed near the main gate and other items displayed in the small museum contained in the gate lodge.

In accordance with their founding Quaker principles, Fry's always envisaged that the development would provide housing and recreation facilities as well as production. They built a total of some sixty houses (at and close to Chandos Road), a large dining hall, playing fields and tennis courts. This provision of accommodation, entertainment, sport and education for employees was years ahead of its time and these activities were increased over the ensuing years to play an important part in the life of Keynsham. Many employees and Keynsham residents in general had good reason to look back on these early days with respect and many happy memories.

In 1923 a competition was held nationally to choose a name for the new venture and a staggering 173,000 entries were received. The winning suggestion of "Somerdale" had been made by a total of 120 competitors and the original prize of £500 had to be split, with each winning £5. A second phase of development was carried out between 1931 and 1938 with further ranges of manufacturing blocks and an impressive administration block. By 1935 all production had been moved from Bristol and a total of 6,000 worked at

An aerial view of Somerdale, probably taken in 1932

Somerdale.

The management at Fry's under the leadership of Cecil Fry and Egbert Cadbury were never slow to seize an opportunity for publicity and, recognizing the current vogue for air travel, leased a De Havilland DH 80A Puss Moth. The inaugural flight in September 1932 attracted great media attention, being mentioned in 127 newspapers and periodicals, but by February 1933 the aircraft was on loan to 'The Houston Mount Everest Expedition'. After it returned from this, little more is known about the use of the plane. Much more successful was the 'Fry's Show Train' comprising three carriages painted in a livery of royal blue and gold which, from May 1933, toured the country promoting the company's products and carrying two salesmen who lived on board. Although primarily for trade customers, members of the public were allowed to visit at certain times and were given free samples. The train continued in use until the outbreak of the Second World War when it was decommissioned and offered to the GWR.

However, all the publicity stunts couldn't disguise the fact that the company was losing money – its own and Cadbury's – and the matter was brought to a head in 1933 when Fry's made a loss of £22,787. The board of Cadbury's therefore decided on a major restructuring, putting J S Fry and Sons into liquidation in December 1935, keeping Cecil Fry as a figurehead Managing Director with Egbert Cadbury effectively running the business on behalf of Cadbury's Ltd.

'THE WAR YEARS'

The outbreak of the Second World War in 1939 brought great changes to Somerdale, that would last for the next six years. Signage was removed from the buildings, the 'Somerdale' lettering on the main railway embankment was camouflaged and the railway loading deck completely enclosed. Windows were blacked out and all buildings were protected with banks of sandbags; the grounds were ploughed up to form giant vegetable beds. An ARP (Air Raid Precautions) unit was stationed on the top of

September 1939 - Gas masks being assembled

October 1939 - Sand bags protect C Block

March 1940 - Ploughing to create the kitchen garden

C Block whilst the basement was used as an air-raid shelter for the workers; a Home Guard division was formed at the factory. There was also a Decontamination Group in case of gas attack and staff were instructed in basic first aid. Sweet rationing and the shortage of raw materials led the company to scale-down its production of chocolate and to focus instead on cocoa, which was a much-needed commodity.

From 1941, small vans were sent out

to Portsmouth and Plymouth bomb-sites and victims of the Blitz in Bath and Bristol to distribute hot cocoa. A large portion of the Somerdale buildings were commandeered for the war effort with the Bristol Aeroplane Company setting up what was thought to

August 1940 - In the Air-raid Shelter in C Block basement

be the largest drawing office in the world in C Block. Part of the factory was turned over to the manufacture of aircraft components. Somerdale itself was hit by a bomb, which fortunately failed to explode. When the war ended in 1945, Fry's produced special VR chocolate that was sent to children in occupied countries. A total of 29 former employees lost their lives in conflict; their names are included on the factory war memorial.

'ONWARDS AND UPWARDS?'

Following the war, Fry's fortunes took an upturn with an increased share of the home market, with Chocolate Cream and Crunchie leading the way, and by the time sweet rationing finally ended in 1953 the company was looking to expand. Unfortunately, Cecil Fry did not see this development as, after 43 years of service, he died in 1952. In order to meet the increased consumer demand, two-fifths of production had to be made on night-shifts and in 1956 a new block (D Block) was constructed at a cost of £1,200,000. Production of cocoa and chocolate spread was transferred to the Midlands and packaging was now being supplied to Somerdale instead of being manufactured and assembled on site. This freed up valuable space which was converted to a production line to keep pace with increased demand, particularly for the Crunchie bar and Fry's Chocolate Cream,

which continued to enjoy rising sales.

In 1957 Somerdale employed 5,120 workers, many of whom now lived in Keynsham, but the good days were not to last. Production quality problems dogged certain lines and sales reflected the fact. New lines hastily introduced to address the problem only exacerbated it, and in 1963 factory output was no higher than it had been in 1960; in fact it was only 4%

Nut Roasting 1951

Wrapping Crunchie Bars 1956

higher than in 1956, which made the capital investment in a new production line look extremely foolish. Matters were not helped when a sales tax was introduced which depressed chocolate sales even further. The final building on the Somerdale site took place in 1963 when the Fry Hall was opened as an amenity building. This was also the year when Egbert Cadbury retired from the company after nearly 44 years' service.

Packing Easter Eggs 1960

In 1968, the catastrophic floods that affected Keynsham so badly had little effect on the factory itself, with only the basement of the office block being flooded. A photograph taken at the time shows the factory site apparently standing on an island

The Somerdale site stands above the floodwater

surrounded by water. As the Keynsham Hams had historically been flooded at intervals, the initial survey carried out in 1921 had included checks on the old flooding records and had led to a recommendation to build at what proved to be a safe level.

Nonetheless, the flood had a short-term impact on the running of the factory due to the disruption of road access caused by the collapsed bridges. In addition, the Works Fire Brigade, which was a volunteer force drawn from employees, was at the disposal of the County Fire Brigade for outside calls. It was able to provide vital assistance during the flood and members helped to rescue people trapped in their houses at Dapps Hill. The company helped those affected in other ways and a large number of flood-soaked carpets were brought to the factory to be dried out for local families.

The early 1970s saw Fry's become subsumed by Cadbury's, with the name little used. Although it was made at Somerdale, the highly successful Curly Wurly bar was marketed under the Cadbury's label; the Somerdale operation was a shrinking proportion of an expanding group. The company had acquired Pascall Murray in 1964 and in 1969 merged with Schweppes, so was well-represented in the world of soft drinks and confectionery, with brands such as Trebor Bassett and Sharp's Toffee also part of the business.

'DEATH BY A THOUSAND CUTS'

During the 1970s a number of administrative departments were moved to Bournville and most production material was now delivered in bulk by road, which necessitated the installation of huge storage silos. All rail transport ceased, with track being taken up and the Hunslet diesel engine, which had replaced the original Sentinel shunter in 1956, sold for scrap. In 1983 the Fire Brigade was disbanded, with some of its antique equipment sold to collectors and industrial museums.

By the end of the decade, the workforce at Somerdale had been reduced to 2,600 and Cadbury's started to contract the site, with the office block being put up for sale in 1982. In the same year it was also decided to remove the large Fry's sign which had been in place on the

Chocolate Crumb Tanker, used to bring material into Somerdale from factories at Marlbook and Frampton-on-Severn

south face of C Block for forty years and replace it with an equally large Cadbury's sign, as the Fry's name was seen as *an historical oddity with no great commercial value*. The only good news was that the thriving social club would retain its name as the Fry Club.

The news in 1988 that, following major investment in new plant, the remaining workforce would be cut to just 800 over the next five years caused understandable dismay in the community and when

Despite the shrinking workforce, Somerdale celebrated 250 years since the start of Fry's with this float at the Keynsham carnival in 1978

the Fry Hall was closed the same year it marked the end of an era for Keynsham and the role the company played in the community. Since it had been built, the hall had been an important asset in the town, used as a conference and visitor centre and later as a community hall. It was converted into a canteen and office space but not before the Fry Club performed one last pantomime at the venue.

With a reduced product line and a steadily shrinking workforce, the Somerdale site was becoming too big for purpose and outlying buildings were progressively demolished including the gate-house which housed the museum; the contents of this were given to Wansdyke District Council for safekeeping. As

Demolition of the elegant Avonfields House administration block in 1988

The twisted remains of D Block in January 2014

The landmark chimney reaches the end of its life on 19 February 2016

the old office block failed to attract a buyer, it, too, was demolished and even the company soccer pitches were hired out for a short time to the then-homeless Bristol Rovers FC. At about this time, the Ministry of Defence was looking at options for its new procurement headquarters; Somerdale was given serious consideration as the location, but the proposal came to nothing.

By the mid-1990s the range of products was so small that questions were now being asked in Cadbury's boardroom about the continuing viability of the factory, as the company was coming under increased pressure from shareholders. The outcome was that, in October 2007, Cadbury announced that the phased closure of Somerdale would commence in 2009, with production being transferred abroad, resulting in full closure in 2010. There was a hope that this decision might be reversed when, in 2009, Cadbury Plc was taken over by American-based Kraft Foods but, a week after completing the deal, Kraft announced that the planned closure would go ahead. The final production line at Somerdale – Double Decker – made its last bars at 3.30pm on 13 January 2011, with many employees quietly following the final production to the end of the line. Only memories and souvenirs were left.

'REBIRTH'

Following the final closure in April 2011, production equipment was removed and either transferred to other Cadbury factories or sold for scrap and rumours were rife over the future

TRAJECTUS

Prior to the redevelopment, the whole Somerdale site was subject to extensive archaeological evaluation. Evidence was uncovered of what is almost certainly the 'lost' Roman town of Trajectus (Latin for 'bridgehead'). This town or settlement was recorded as a north-south crossing point over the River Avon in the fourth century but its location has never been known. Remains of several buildings, a road network and large quantities of pottery were unearthed.

SOME SOMERDALE PRODUCTS FROM THE 1950S TO THE 1970S

of the site. These rumours were resolved when developer Taylor Wimpey unveiled plans for a mixed development of 700 houses, light industry, retail units, nursing home, health centre and a school and, following eighteen months of planning and public consultation, outline planning permission was granted in September 2013. Demolition of parts of the factory that could not be re-used began almost immediately.

It was expected that the entire project would take up to ten years to complete but the first residents arrived in their new homes in May 2014, giving the site a whole new lease of life.

2014
ROMAN MOSAICS DISPLAYED AT LAST

The Roman mosaics unearthed at the Durley Hill villa site in the 1920s are one of Keynsham's treasures. When the town's new library opened in 2014, as part of the Civic Centre complex, it incorporated, beneath a glass section of the floor, a display of several of the finest of these – properly arranged for the first time in about 1,600 years. The story of their discovery is worth retelling!

When the Parish Church needed a new cemetery, land was purchased at Durley Hill. In 1877 construction of the mortuary chapel foundations revealed the base of masonry walls and floor fragments. Later, the gravediggers grumbled constantly about having to break through a layer of stone and fine pieces of tile. But it was not until 1922, when construction of the Somerdale factory revealed a small Roman villa, that interest was awakened and it was decided to properly research and excavate the site, which archaeologists could easily identify as of Roman origin. By then of course, irreparable damage had been done.

The excavation, funded by Fry's, revealed what was thought to be one of the largest and finest Roman villas in Britain. It extended under the embankment carrying the Bristol Road and it was on the far side of this that the floor of an unusual hexagonal room was discovered with a large and relatively undamaged mosaic floor of the highest quality, with depictions of scenes from the Greek legends. These were salvaged and a home was found for them in the Fry's Museum at the entrance to Somerdale. When that was demolished they were put into store in the Town Hall basement. The late Charles Browne, with others, campaigned tirelessly for the mosaics to be permanently displayed in the town and the North Wansdyke (later

Europa and the Bull

Surrounding segments showed birds and fruits

Keynsham) Heritage Trust was set up to build a museum which would have these as its centrepiece. A design was drawn up for a building at the top of Dapps Hill, but funding was never secured. Construction of the Civic Centre provided an opportunity to display some of the area's historic artefacts and archaeology and the present display was the outcome.

2015
KEYNSHAM CIVIC CENTRE OPENS

The proposal for a new Civic Centre first surfaced seriously in 2011. Bath & North East Somerset Council wanted to bring as many staff as possible onto a single site and make better use of the town centre location. After much debate a management team was appointed and public consultation revealed generally positive reactions. A library and leisure facilities were seen as top priorities and the town's Transition Group called for a sustainable project.

The office blocks take shape in October 2013

In January 2012, Wilmott Dixon was awarded the contract and the library moved to temporary accommodation. The proposed design was controversial: in May, English Heritage condemned it and a Civic Society poll showed five for and 250 against. Planning approval was given for a slightly modified (that is, lower) building in November. By then, demolition of the existing buildings had begun and local businesses were being encouraged to tender for services.

The old Town Hall and clock tower disappeared early in 2013. Progress in building was soon visible with the steel frame being completed in August. Proposals were made for an art installation and a giant advertising video screen. A 'topping out' ceremony took place on the last day in October – yew tree branch placed, wine, oil, corn and salt sprinkled.

On 16 January 2014, the giant crane which had dominated the town came down. The cladding of the new blocks, intended to recall the local brass industry, was initially very bright and came in for much criticism. Details and artwork were being consulted on and street names decided. The video screen was dropped but public requests for a new clock led to a competition: Sebastian Boysen's design was chosen in June.

The Library opened first, in October 2014, incorporating a 'One Stop Shop' with a police enquiry desk; from January 2015 Film Works moved its screenings to The Space but take-up of the retail units was slow. In April 2015 the Centre was short-listed for a RIBA sustainability award, which it duly won. The new clock tower was initiated in September and Pomegranate opened a new restaurant in November. Work was almost finished and the main building was to be handed over by the end of the year. The new Civic Centre had arrived.

Later, in September 2016, a time capsule containing photographs, local publications, Town Council papers and items from local clubs and groups was placed under a paving slab on the steps below Bonzo Lounge and an inscribed slab unveiled to mark the spot.

2018
THE NEW SOMERDALE OPENS

The redevelopment of the Somerdale site was a huge project and of great importance to Keynsham. In 2013 the site was sold to Taylor Wimpey, who started immediately on the construction of houses on the land on the west side of Somerdale Drive. The first residents arrived in 2014 and on completion this area contained some 230 properties, with roads named after Roman emperors in a nod to the prehistory of the site.

To accommodate the house-building programme and comply with a commitment given by Kraft, a new Pavilion was one of the first new structures in the scheme. This was completed in 2015, including a gym, changing rooms, bar and a range of rooms for events and meetings; the old Fry Club building could then be demolished. It guaranteed the continuation of the playing field as an asset for local sports teams such as the Fry Club FC.

Always the most visible parts of the factory, the main iconic redbrick blocks were subsequently sold on to be developed into a £60million retirement complex by St Monica's Trust and a competition was held to choose a name. This was won by Keynsham resident and former Fry's employee, Donald Ogg, with 'The Chocolate Quarter' which truly reflects the history of Somerdale and its place in Keynsham life. The formal opening ceremony was performed by HRH The Princess Royal on 13 April 2018.

This part of the site includes one block of 136 retirement flats (formerly A Block), and a care home, named Charterhouse, for up to 77 residents (B Block) with café, restaurant and extensive leisure facilities on the ground floor. These include a cinema, swimming pool, hair and beauty salon, and an art and pottery studio.

Laying the Foundation Stone on 11 January 2016, left to right Cosmo Fry, Sir David Wills (Patron of St Monica Trust) and David Williams (Chief Executive of the Trust)

Relocation of the St Augustine's Medical Practice to C Block means that residents also have healthcare on site.

St Monica's Trust continued to expand its role at the site and in 2019 reached a deal to take over the Somerdale Pavilion from Mondelez (formerly Kraft) and incorporate the management into its other activities. Early in 2020 it was announced that they had purchased more land from Taylor Wimpey and would be developing this to provide another thirty-six retirement homes.

A key aspect of the redevelopment at the planning stage was the conversion of C Block to provide office accommodation. By early 2020 almost all the 87,000 sq ft (8,000 sq m) of this had been let with tenants including Pukka Herbs, Independent Vetcare and facilities management company Mitie, together bringing several hundred permanent jobs to the site. So, a new generation of people are working in the redbrick blocks!

2019
FRY'S SENTINEL STEAMS AGAIN

When the Somerdale factory was built, much of its input and output went by rail. The factory had two-and-a-half miles of track connected to the main line at Keynsham Station. Fry's needed a shunting engine to move wagons within the site and bought one in 1928 from the Sentinel Waggon Works in Shrewsbury. They chose this type because it was similar in operation to the Sentinel steam lorries they used at the time. For a railway locomotive it was small, and unusual in having a vertical boiler.

The Sentinel gave many years of service and Bill Payne was its driver until he retired in 1946. Gladstone Hendy took over until 1956, when the Sentinel was retired and a new diesel shunter took over.

The two engines shared a shed until 1964 when the Sentinel was sold for £50 to Grove scrap merchants of Fishponds, Bristol. However, instead of being cut up it was put on display there until 1970, when it was bought by Mr A P Gardiner of Tunley. Later, it went to a Mr Finbow of Bacton in Suffolk and then, in 1991, to Steve Wood of Wix in Essex, who built a shed for it in his garden.

In 2005, Eric Miles, a former Fry's employee, who had memories of riding on the loco in his youth, started on a mission to find the Sentinel. After much detective work he tracked it down. On 1 May 2009 he visited Steve Wood and saw the Sentinel for the first time since 1956. Surprisingly, it was virtually complete and Steve was of the opinion that it should be restored.

Eric's next port of call was the Avon Valley Railway (AVR), where he thought it might find a new home and be restored. Although keen to have the engine, AVR had no funds, so Eric approached Cadbury's management who agreed to pay for its purchase and transport.

On 4 September 2010 the Sentinel was craned out of its shed in Essex and put on a low-loader for its journey to the AVR, making a sentimental call at Somerdale on the way. Years of work followed, mainly by volunteers under the guidance of AVR engineer Jon Miles. The boiler was repaired and re-tubed; J R Goold Restorations of Camerton, the country's leading Sentinel experts, manufactured a new superheater coil and overhauled all the boiler fittings. The Sentinel Drivers' Club also provided much valuable help.

Finally, Easter 2019 saw the Sentinel steaming again at its triumphant public launch. Four days of glorious weather made the event a great success with the engine giving brake-van rides and getting much publicity. It was a sight for sore eyes for many retired Fry's workers!

A painting by Alan Ward of the Sentinel when new, in 1928

2020
LAUNCH OF RADIO STATION KTCRfm

Since 2014, KTCR, Keynsham's local radio, has produced the weekly 'Keynsham Hour' from a studio in Community at 67 on Queens Road. It was broadcast on Somer Valley FM each Thursday and was then available as a podcast on the station's website. The experience gained through the relationship with Somer Valley FM was the first step in creating a community-based local station for Keynsham.

Keynsham Town Community Radio (KTCR) Ltd was set up in 2017 to respond to Ofcom's invitation to apply for community radio licences. Ric Davison, Keynsham Music Festival organizer, and Seb Bailey, who provided technical expertise, coordinated the rigorous application process. They were backed up by an advisory board which included Stephen Rodgers of *The Week In*, Dom Chambers of Somer Valley FM, Mike Corrigan of Keynsham Talking Newspaper and Ian Aitchison, owner of Longwell Records.

In November 2017, Keynsham was successful in being awarded one of nine community licences granted by Ofcom. They commented: "........The applicant has links with a range of local organizations and individuals, and provided evidence of demand and support for the proposed service."

Community radio services are provided on a not-for-profit basis, focusing on the delivery of specific social benefits to a particular community. Project funding has come from the National Lottery, the Quartet Foundation and Keynsham Town Council.

Once the licence was granted, a great deal of work was involved in locating and building

Fitting out the new studio at One Community Trust

a studio and transmission site, as well as training presenters and sourcing programme material. The transmitter, erected in Burnett, was found to reach communities both nearby and further afield, giving 100,000 people access to the station. In January 2020 it began test transmissions on 105.80FM. A landmark was achieved on Thursday 30 January 2020, when the Keynsham Hour magazine programme was broadcast simultaneously on Somer Valley FM and on KTCRfm. Valentine's Day was another first when locally-made programmes with a love theme were broadcast throughout the day.

From the third week in February 2020, the station was broadcasting twenty-four seven and moving towards producing at least three hours of local programmes daily, either live or pre-recorded. All programmes are made by volunteer contributors who either live locally or have links to the town.

This latest step in the history of the district has provided a new way of helping people through the difficulties of coronavirus as this text is concluded in April 2020.

PART 2
LIVES AND TIMES

CHAPTER I
SOME LOCAL PERSONALITIES

GEORGE ASHTON
1904 – 1980

When Ashton Way was opened in 1975 it was named after George Reginald Ashton, who was Clerk to Keynsham Urban District Council from its formation in 1938 until his retirement in 1969. It is unusual for a public servant to be recognized in this way and the honour is a measure of the esteem in which George Ashton was held. His position was what today would be described as Chief Executive and he was a man of considerable energy and ability. Keynsham was not a town that was large or particularly noteworthy but throughout the post-war period it was modernized in various respects. Whilst fifty years later the widespread demolition of old properties is often viewed as a mistake, at the time it was seen as essential to progress. Under George Ashton's guidance, the Council removed many houses that were in poor condition and unfit for habitation, it built the Memorial Park, the Town Hall and adjacent shops and the Leisure Centre. After starting his career as an office junior in a Lancashire council office on 10s [50p] a week he progressed to Deputy Clerk at Whitefield Urban Council before being selected from seventy applicants for the post of Clerk at Keynsham at the age of 34.

As well as his professional work, George Ashton was also prominent locally and in the trade union world. In 1955 he was President of Keynsham Rotary Club and he was an active member of the National and Local Government Officers' Association, known as NALGO. In 1940 he founded the North Somerset branch of the Association and joined the South Western District committee in 1941, becoming a member of the National Executive in 1947. He later spent four years chairing the committee that negotiated staff salaries nationally and became President of the Association in 1962. This was a time when the public sector was expanding in both size and importance and NALGO was one of the major white-collar unions, with membership approaching 300,000. Mr. Ashton said that he had two ambitions during his term of office. They were to win for all members "the salaries they merit" and to see the Association's membership reach 300,000. The latter was quickly achieved when the British Gas Staff Association was absorbed into NALGO, taking the total to over 310,000.

When his retirement was announced, in 1968, the Chairman of the UDC, Councillor Pestridge, said "...we are seeing the end of an era of outstanding service and devotion, not only in Keynsham, but across a much wider area."

George Ashton was awarded the MBE in 1950 for his work as Local Fuel Overseer and the OBE in 1969 for co-ordinating the flood relief efforts the previous year.

BILL BAILEY
B 1965

Born Mark Robert Bailey in 1965, Bill Bailey is with little doubt Keynsham's best-known face in the world of modern entertainment, although he makes little mention of his west country origins. Bill is the son of Dr Christopher Bailey who was a much-respected GP in the town for many years until his retirement. His mother was a ward sister at the Royal United Hospital in Bath. The family home was at the bottom of Wellsway, where his father's surgery comprised two rooms until he moved to new premises at Temple Street.

The breadth of Bill's talent became apparent during his teenage years at King Edward's School, Bath. He won prizes in academic subjects but soon discovered the excitement of performing as a member of the school band. Entertaining was in his blood and he often combined music with sport by leading the singing on the coach trips back from away rugby fixtures. It is said that he was given the nickname Bill by his music teacher, for being able to play the old song *"Won't you come home Bill Bailey"* so well on the guitar. After leaving school he studied English but did not pursue this for long, as the attraction of music and comedy proved too strong.

He trained in classical music at the London College of Music but by the age of twenty Bill had begun touring the country as a stand-up comedian as part of a double act. He soon began to develop his own style, mixing music and a whimsical humour, with fact and fiction sometimes indistinguishable.

In 1994 Bill teamed up with Sean Lock for their Edinburgh show *Rock*, before taking his first solo show, *Cosmic Jam*, to the Edinburgh Festival Fringe in 1995 and earning a Perrier nomination the following year. 1998 saw the BBC give him his own television show *Is It Bill Bailey?* in which he wrote and presented

At the Royal Albert Hall, 2008 Photo: Nick Webb, Wikimedia Commons

a mixture of musical parodies and surreal sketches. After this breakthrough he won the Best Live Stand-Up award in the British Comedy Awards in 1999. In the following years he made guest appearances in various shows including *Room 101*, *Spaced* and *Have I Got News For You*. He appeared in the pilot of the panel game *QI* in 2003 and many episodes since. Bill took over as team captain on *Never Mind the Buzzcocks* in 2002 and remained in the captain's chair for eleven series before departing in 2008.

In recent years Bill has appeared on a remarkably wide range of other shows, including wildlife and birdwatching, as either performer or presenter. His television work is combined with a schedule of live performances; as one of the country's top stand-up comedians Bill now tours the country and the world, his 2018-2020 show being named *Larks in Transit*.

PERCY BAKER
1905 – 1991

A Keynsham man through and through, Percy Baker had a prominent role in the life of the town for many years.

Born in 1905 in a cottage in the fields at the bottom of Durley Hill, he was the youngest of seven, and went to school at Temple Street and then Bath Hill. Too young to be involved in the First World War, he lost two of his brothers in the conflict. He left school at fourteen and was apprenticed to a ladies and gents tailor in Bath. In 1926 the business closed, and he went into business in Bath with a colleague. The hours were long and he recalled that sometimes he had to work late into the night to finish work for a client on time.

In 1927, Percy decided that he could find sufficient business on his own, so he dissolved the partnership and opened a shop above the saddler's in Keynsham High Street. He married the following year and in 1929 went to live over a shop in the High Street, in a rented property. At first, there was no shop window so he had to leave the door open. Later a shop front was installed so he ran the business from there until 1950.

In 1945 he bought another outfitter's business on the opposite side near the Fear Institute - a lock-up shop – and kept both going for a period before concentrating on the newer one. At his retirement, he had been in business for 46 years and his shop was an established part of the High Street.

After encouragement from Dr Claude Harrison, in 1957 Percy stood successfully as an Independent for election to Keynsham UDC and served for seventeen years, becoming chairman or vice-chairman of most of the committees over the years. He was the driving force in the building of the town's swimming pool and was the last Chairman of the Council, being in office at its abolition in 1974.

Percy had many other roles in the town, serving as chairman of the Keynsham Charities and a governor of several schools. His interests included bowling and running the Keynsham Men's Fireside Fellowship, a social group formed about 1934, which lasted until the 1980s.

Shop near the Fear Hall in 1965

HORACE BATCHELOR
1898 - 1977

The name "Keynsham" achieved a unique place in the memories of a generation of teenagers and young people in 1960s Britain due to the advertising campaign of one man – Horace Batchelor – for his business of 'investing' on the football pools, which he called the Infra-Draw Method, of which he was the inventor and sole proprietor.

Born in Bristol in 1898, in his early life Horace was a market trader, barrow boy and general dealer selling cigarettes and toothpaste, amongst other things. In 1948,

The start of the Introductory Letter to subscribers

he had the good fortune to win £12,563 on the football pools, which in post-war Britain were a popular way of gambling small stakes on the results of games in the four divisions of the Football League. All weekend matches were played on a Saturday afternoon, with kick-off at 3.00pm, and up to fifteen million people played 'The Pools' every week.

Horace was an astute businessman and saw an opportunity to turn his good luck into a thriving football pools system, which he promoted as an investment plan.

The basis of the plan was that, every week, he would make an entry in the largest seven Treble Chance Pools in the country with his 7-from-12 permutation entering 792 lines at 1/- [5p] each, total £39 12s 0d [£39.60]. He needed to recruit 40 members at £1/per head, or proportionately more members for smaller stakes, to raise the £39 12s 0d stake and the permutations would be entered on their behalf. He said that the actual matches selected for the Treble Chance entry would be based on the Infra-Draw calculations;

how he chose them is not clear, but later he had an electro-mechanical machine made to suggest a technical input.

Other than the stake money, there was no charge to participate, but Horace took 1/- [5p] in the £ commission on all the Infra-Draw clients' winnings. Due to the large number of lines entered, there would frequently be winners. In the years following the start of the plan winnings for his clients increased steadily as more people enrolled, rather than submitting their stakes to the pools companies direct. Total winnings were over £75,000 in the 1949-1950 season, and in the following years £120,000, £185,000 and over £325,000. By the 1954-1955 season the plan was generating over £600,000 in winnings for clients.

To achieve and maintain this growth, a substantial outlay on advertising was necessary. In an era when the BBC was the only broadcaster in Britain – there were no commercial stations – Horace Batchelor decided to put a significant part of his advertising effort into sponsoring programmes on Radio Luxembourg, a pioneering commercial radio station which had been transmitting to Britain and Ireland from mainland Europe since 1933. The station was popular, especially with young people who wanted to listen to the latest pop music: tuning the transistor radio to "208 metres on the medium wave-band" was routine entertainment.

Through the 1950s and 1960s up to 1971 the advertisements for Infra-Draw were a constant feature of the Luxembourg output. The reason they achieved such a high profile, and became almost part of the language, was that respondents had to send their stakes to Horace Batchelor in Keynsham. Because the name is not pronounced as it appears, it was spelled out: K-E-Y-N-S-H-A-M. This became ingrained in the listeners' minds so that almost everyone in the country over a certain age still knows it by heart. For many it triggers fond memories of teenage years spent listening to the radio under the bed clothes.

To become a success Horace Batchelor also had to run an efficient business. His clients would receive a copy of their entry every Tuesday for the following Saturday's matches and any winnings due were always sent out on the following Wednesday. At the height of his success, several sack-loads of post were delivered every day, with each letter containing a postal order to buy a portion of the Infra-Draw submission. He won many large amounts and

The Random Selection Machine, now owned by Bristol Museum

he had the cheques of his winnings photocopied to be used for publicity.

Horace entertained many famous people, including stars from Radio Luxembourg, at his home on Bath Road between Keynsham and Saltford. When he purchased it in the 1950s, he renamed the house Infra Grange, although after his death it reverted to its original name of Long Reach House; it then had several uses before conversion to residential flats.

During an interesting life, in which he acquired substantial wealth from his business, Horace Batchelor later supported many good causes and at his death in 1977 he left the bulk of his estate to be equally divided between a range of charities.

LUCY MIDDLETON (NÉE COX)
1894 - 1983

Lucy Middleton was a remarkable and principled woman who devoted most of her life to furthering the political ideals of pacificism and socialism that she believed in so passionately.

Born on 9 May 1894 as Lucy Annie Cox, she was the second daughter of Sidney Cox and his wife Ada. Her father was a wire drawer at the Keynsham Brass Mills and the family lived at 16 Albert Road, Keynsham. Lucy entered Keynsham Primary School in February 1901 and gained a scholarship in 1908 to study at Colston Girls' School in Bristol. This was followed by a scholarship to become a pupil teacher and, following training at Bristol University, she taught for ten years in various schools.

From her father, Lucy had developed a strong interest in radical politics and in 1916 she joined the Independent Labour Party (ILP). After three years she became secretary of the Keynsham branch, attending the annual conferences, and moved upwards through the organization. Deeply affected by the slaughter of the First World War she became increasingly involved in pacifism and as well as working for the ILP, Lucy joined the No-More-War movement and travelled around the country speaking at rallies on its behalf. By September 1924 Lucy had become the Organizing Secretary of the movement and the next year General Secretary in which capacity she continued into the 1930s.

Leaving the pacifist movement to concentrate on party politics, she decided it was time to try to become a Member of Parliament, at a time when female candidates were few and far between (it was only two years since the franchise had been extended to all women), and stood unsuccessfully for Labour in Sevenoaks in 1931, followed by several other

Lucy Middleton née Cox, c 1950
© National Portrait Gallery, London

contests before becoming MP for Plymouth Sutton, as one of the fifteen women elected in the Labour landslide of 1945. The focus of her interest remained very much on international affairs but she found time occasionally to raise issues relevant to her Somerset birthplace, as in 1947 when she asked the Minister of Transport "when is it expected that work will be commenced on the proposed new section of the Bristol-Bath road to by-pass the village of Keynsham?"

She lost her seat in Plymouth in 1951 and failed to regain it in 1955. Nevertheless she remained active for the rest of her life, advising the Labour government and running the charity War on Want for ten years from 1958.

MARY FAIRCLOUGH
1913 -1999

When Mary Fairclough died on New Year's Eve 1999 at the age of 86, Keynsham lost one of its most talented and spirited residents.

Mary was born into the Thomas family, her grandfather being William Thomas of St Augustine's, Station Road, who was, with his brother Alfred Thomas of Saltford, the owner of Albert Mill in Dapps Hill, commonly known as the Logwood Mill, and she spent her whole life in the town. She had great talent as an artist using various media, being described variously as a painter, printmaker, illustrator and potter. After studying at home with Katherine Gunton for several years, she attended part-time at the West of England Art College in Bristol. Her work was shown at the Clifton Arts Club, the Ward Gallery and the Royal West of England Academy. Commercially, she worked for Macmillan and several other publishers, illustrating children's books.

In 1946, Mary painted a remarkable map for Keynsham's first Children's Library; this featured landmarks and characters to help tell the town's story across the centuries. This map has survived several changes of building and now hangs on the first floor of the Library building opened in 2014.

Mary's art was very varied, including miniatures and paintings on large pebbles gathered from the beach near Dunster, where she spent many holidays. She could see images in the shapes and would paint them in poster colours, sealed with varnish to produce what she

Map of Keynsham, painted in 1946

St Keyna

called 'Cloughstones'.

As well as an artist, Mary was a writer and a photographer, but her passion was history and especially local history. Her knowledge of the story of Keynsham was unrivalled and she was a founder member of both the Keynsham & Saltford Local History Society and the Keynsham Civic Society. Indeed, the Civic Society was formed when Mary and others were horrified at the demolition of the little cottages in Temple Street prior to the building of the large office block, which she would have described as 'egg-box' development, and determined to do something to prevent similar destruction in future. After thorough research, she then put together the first list of Keynsham's important buildings, helping to gain them listed status,

and in the 1970s pushed for the Conservation Area that now safeguards buildings in Dapps Hill and nearby.

She was always delighted to share her knowledge with others and gave lectures and commentaries on the history of the area. Many of her photographs survive, with descriptions on the back describing snippets of history that would otherwise have been lost.

One of Mary's endearing characteristics was a wicked sense of humour, which she enjoyed directing at pomposity. This extended to her art, with a marvellous cartoon painting highlighting the threat to little Keynsham from the tentacles of the octopus monsters of Bristol on one side and Bath on the other.

Mary Fairclough was not only an active campaigner, committee member and historian but also a very popular one. After her death many tributes were paid and she is remembered fondly by all who knew her.

In 2015, former colleagues from the Civic Society mounted an exhibition of Mary's art works at The Space above the library bringing together as many examples as they could find, as a tribute to her. These included a selection of her lino-cuts and two of these are shown above.

DR CLAUDE CHARLES HARRISON
1890 -1957

Keynsham born and bred, 'Dr Claude' as he was affectionately known, descended from a family of doctors including his own father, the redoubtable Dr Charles, a well-known and loved Keynsham doctor. His uncle, by marriage, was the famous cricketer, Dr W G Grace.

He served as a major in the Royal Army Medical Corps during the First World War and was mentioned in dispatches and awarded the Military Cross. On his return to Keynsham in 1920 he lost no time in helping to re-form the Keynsham Cricket Club and was recognized as a talented player. Over the years he fulfilled many roles for the club as captain, secretary, chairman and president and most importantly as a trustee when the club took on a mortgage to purchase the new ground in 1930. Claude subsequently took over the mortgage himself, paying it off in 1939 and gifted a plot of land to form the entrance from the Wellsway.

During the Second World War he organized baseball matches for the American troops stationed at Burnett at the ground, a great novelty at the time, and many a Keynsham youngster was introduced to popcorn and the music of Glenn Miller at these events. He had a keen interest in many sports and was also president of the Keynsham Rugby Club, a position he held from 1928 to 1956. He also was an enthusiastic amateur actor, taking part in many productions given by 'Whittucks Company', often in the Drill Hall, to raise funds for community projects.

In 1923 he joined his father Dr Charles Harrison at his surgery in Tregare House, 44 High Street (now the site of the Post Office) and ministered to the needs of local people for the rest of his life. Local resident Hazel Cannock remembers there being an open fire in the surgery with a cat curled up in front of it – a far cry from today's more clinical surgeries! In the days before the National Health Service, doctors' visits and treatments had to be paid for but many a family had cause to be grateful to 'Dr Claude' as he continued his father's tradition of not charging those in genuine hardship. In addition to his General Practice workload, he was also a police doctor and Medical Officer at the Workhouse, a connection which was later commemorated by the ward named after him at Keynsham Hospital.

After his death in 1957, the main gates to Memorial Park were refurbished in his memory and a memorial plaque reads 'A much loved doctor and sporting enthusiast who devoted his life to the welfare of Keynsham people'.

CHRISTINA HOLLIS
B 1959

Christina Hollis (a nom de plume) was born in Keynsham and attended Wellsway School. The Careers Department suggested nursing or teaching but all she had ever wanted to do was to write. After leaving school she worked at first in finance and marketing but quickly found that she preferred words to spreadsheets. After meeting her husband on a blind date, she lived in Bristol for a period before moving to the Gloucestershire countryside. She then began writing full-time about natural history and life in the country and was successful in having pieces published in magazines such as *The Garden* and *The Lady*.

At the same time, in her 'spare' time she was working on her first full-length fiction book.

This first novel, '*Knight's Pawn*', was published under another name in 1990. After taking a break to raise her family Christina enrolled on a creative-writing course where she discovered how to write short stories and began to write contemporary romance. She has found great success in this field, with some eighteen books to her name, some translated into twenty languages, and total sales of around three million. More recently, Christina has written on the more serious subject of '*Struggle and Suffrage in Bristol*', published in 2019.

RICHARD SMITH
B 1963

Richard was born in 1963 and moved to Keynsham five years later. He attended Chandag Infant School and Wellsway School until 1981, before moving to London to study law at King's College, University of London. Richard qualified as a barrister in 1986 after further studies in Bristol, later being appointed to the position of Queen's Counsel in 2001. At the time he was the youngest criminal barrister to be appointed a 'silk', aged just 38. Practising from Guildhall Chambers in Bristol, his practice as a barrister is split between criminal trials and sports law. In respect of the latter, Richard has built an international reputation in representing rugby players at disciplinary hearings. He has been retained as Counsel to the England team since 2003 and has attended the Rugby World Cups in that capacity since then.

Like many young sportsmen developed through the Wellsway School PE department of the 1970s and 1980s, Richard achieved county honours in both rugby and cricket. On leaving school, he graduated to the playing ranks of Keynsham Rugby Club and was a part of the 1981-1982 team that won both the Somerset and Bristol Combination cups. Richard still lives locally; he is married with two children.

BARBARA LOWE
1927 - 2012

Of all the lost buildings of Keynsham, the Abbey was by far the finest and the most important. Our knowledge of this huge part of our heritage is due to one person more than any other: Barbara Lowe, who died on 28 August 2012, at the age of 85.

Barbara was born in Handsworth, Birmingham, but grew up near Taunton. When she was only thirteen, her father died of tuberculosis, making life a struggle for her mother. Barbara looked after her younger brother, Arthur, in the school holidays and to save money, mother and daughter made the family's clothes and soft furnishings, as well as growing vegetables and keeping chickens.

In 1946, Barbara won a scholarship for teacher training at Bristol University, where she studied for a BSc in Maths and Physics. Whilst at Bristol she met Francis Lowe, an ex-bomber pilot and prisoner-of-war, who had come from Oxford to Bristol to help run the family business. They married in 1948 and moved to Manor Road in Keynsham with their two sons in 1955.

Barbara joined a weekly adult educational class in archaeology. This class had a very active offshoot, the Bristol Folk House Archaeological Society, which in the summer months undertook training 'digs' wherever voluntary assistance was required. When the construction of the Keynsham by-pass started in 1964, with its route passing through the site of Keynsham Abbey, the Society was called upon to carry out a rescue dig. Barbara, as a local resident, played a leading role and developed an enthusiasm that changed her life. She collected and recorded items of interest as the earthmovers uncovered them and subsequently was heavily involved in excavating the rest of the site. Barbara also took on the collation and writing up of the results, for publication in the Proceedings of the Somerset Archaeology and Natural History Society (SANHS).

Among the shattered remains of the Abbey were thousands of fragments of medieval floor tiles of various patterns and styles, many from sixteen-piece sets, each bearing parts of the coat of arms of one of the many benefactors of the Abbey. These proved to have particular fascination for Barbara - she had always been keen on jigsaw puzzles, but this was in a different league. She spent a great deal of time over some fifteen years matching up the fragments and writing the definitive work on the Abbey, its history, buildings, floor tiles and artefacts. Her book on the tiles is one of the standard works on the subject and in recognition she was elected a Fellow of the Society of Antiquaries of London, an accolade rarely given to amateur archaeologists.

Working on the Abbey led Barbara to join the newly formed Keynsham & Saltford Local History Society and over the years she made an immense contribution to its work, taking on, amongst other roles, that of photographic archivist and eventually president. The Society has a particularly good selection of aerial photographs of the town, taken by her as she flew with her husband who had maintained his pilot's licence. Having once vowed that she would never join a committee, over the years she joined many, some fifteen in all, and each of them associated with local history or archaeology. She was a particular supporter of SANHS, based in Taunton where she grew up. She also edited various periodicals, was author of seven books and co-author of another ten books and reports. For seventeen years she lectured in adult education and over a period of forty years gave numerous talks on Keynsham Abbey and related topics.

In 1962, Barbara entered the world of work as a laboratory technician at Keynsham Grammar School until, after her boys had finished secondary schooling, she left to study for a B Ed, which enabled her to become a mathematics teacher.

At home, besides archaeology and history, she had a wide range of interests and hobbies, including watercolour painting, making soft furnishings and even wooden furniture. This

Tiles as found in the Abbey nave

was in addition to her beloved embroidery, crochet, knitting and gardening.

Barbara was a very approachable person, always keen to help, with many friends as well as being a devoted mother and wife. In her later years she suffered health problems and the loss of both her husband and younger son, yet continued to lead an active and fulfilling life, including remaining as an active member of the Local History Society committee until shortly before her death.

GEOFF MABBS
1933 - 1983

Geoffrey James Mabbs is remembered not only as the former proprietor of Mabbs' Rock Road garage and a local Keynsham councillor, but also during the 1960s as a successful motor rally racing driver. His career started in the late 1950s when he gained success in the RAC annual GB rally where timed stages of driving were important; it also included special driving tests to examine car-handling skills. These events were in cars which by today's standards were basic, with provision for driver safety that was non-existent.

His passion for motor racing soon took Geoff across Europe where, in Holland, driving a Triumph Herald with co-driver Leslie Griffiths, he gained early success winning the 1961 Tulpenrallye (Tulip Rally), driving the same car later in the Monte Carlo rally.

Geoff was now not only becoming an established rally driver and mixing with the best in Europe, but he was also at the forefront of British motor race engineering in pioneering the development of British-made vehicles. Changes were being made to the engine, bodywork and suspension, converting the basic model into a fast, effective, rally racing car. The original Morris Mini 997cc would soon take the new format of a 1071cc Cooper S, which was subsequently highlighted in the original filming of "*The Italian Job*". In the picture Geoff is driving a Cooper S in the 1963 Monte Carlo rally – he finished a creditable eighteenth.

in 2020, the Cooper S, built by BMW, still has the distinctive Mini body shape but beneath the bonnet there is a 1998cc turbo engine capable of 0-60mph in 6.8secs with a top speed in excess of 140mph. How Geoff would have enjoyed driving this!

His racing career for the BMC works team included performances in the iconic Monte Carlo Rally which, in the 1960s, captured

Mabbs in rally-winning Triumph Herald about 1961

Taking part in the Monte Carlo Rally 1963

In the 1966 Monte Carlo Rally

the imagination of a generation. After 1963, mentioned above, he raced in the 1964, 1965 and 1966 events with his highest placing of tenth coming in the last of these, when he drove a Rover 2000.

Geoff was a familiar face on UK race circuits, in particular on the local race scene at Castle Combe, where much of his race practice and vehicle testing was completed. In September 1965, a car named the Mini Marcos, which had a Mini Cooper S 1,293cc engine and had been built by Janspeed Engineering of Salisbury, made its racing debut in the 1,600cc GT race with Geoff Mabbs at the wheel. After only seven laps of practice, in atrociously wet conditions, he raced into pole position and went on to win by a comfortable margin.

Geoff Mabbs' Garage in 1972 with the new building taking shape behind the old one

Continuing his racing career throughout the 1960s, Geoff maintained his liaison with the Mini Cooper S BMC works team, Janspeed Engineering and Marcos Cars in Westbury, but during the 1970s his garage business became more of a priority, with the old building being demolished and a Ford car dealership established on the new premises.

With some of his trophies

LILIAN SLADE (NÉE NETHERCOTT)
1894 -2003

On 25 May 1894, a remarkable baby, Lilian Nethercott, was born at Clack's Farm in Keynsham Road, Willsbridge. She lived to celebrate her 108th birthday in 2002 in style at her own independent flat, which was in the Gardens Care sheltered housing scheme in School Road, Cadbury Heath, surrounded by her many friends and family. Her grandson, Kelvin, who plays in Bath Spa Brass Band, serenaded her with fellow band members on this special day which she enjoyed enormously.

Lilian, shown seated

Lilian's father, Frederick, was a miller at Clack's Farm where the family lived, and she attended a local school. On leaving school she worked at Carson's Chocolate factory and also was in service to a local family. Although she did not live in Keynsham, Lilian often visited; she enjoyed shopping in the town and especially at a cake shop in the High Street. She also went in later life to the Charlton Cinema twice a week taking Freda, her youngest daughter, with her.

A friend, Elsie, with whom Lilian worked, set her up on a blind date with her brother, so Lilian met Robert George Slade, who came from Westerleigh. He had just returned from France, having been injured in the Battle of the Somme. They married on 1 November 1919 and settled in Westerleigh for a while before moving to a cottage next to "The Queens Head" in Willsbridge. They enjoyed forty happy years together before Lilian was widowed. There were five children: Doris, Cecil, Joe, Betty and Freda but very sadly Doris drowned in the River Avon near The Chequers when she was twelve years old. The couple had twelve grandchildren and twelve great-grandchildren, all of whom gave her great pleasure.

Robert and Lilian made their own ice-cream – said to be delicious - and Robert and Joe used to go around the area in a pony and trap selling it. On one occasion the pony started to bolt with the result that father and son returned to Lilian covered in ice-cream! They also kept a lot of chickens which they sold, especially at Christmas, which of course kept Lilian very busy in plucking them. Towards the end of the Second World War, on a Sunday, the house shook violently: an aeroplane had crash-landed in the garden behind the house. A fire broke out and the family were able to help the pilot, who was not seriously injured.

In old age, Lilian retained her faculties and her sense of humour and way past her 100th birthday she was still knitting and doing crochet. In 2003, she was believed to be the oldest person living in the Bristol region and was close to winning a place in the Guinness Book of records for being the oldest person in Britain!

SIOBHAN-MARIE O'CONNOR
B 1995

Siobhan-Marie O'Connor is one of Great Britain's most successful female swimmers, having won medals at every level of competition, including silver at the 2016 Olympic Games. Siobhan was born in Bath on 29 November 1995 and has been a member of Keynsham Amateur Swimming Club for many years. She attended St Gregory's School in Bath but by the age of fifteen was establishing herself in the world of competitive swimming.

Following encouraging performances at the European Junior Championship in 2010, she burst onto the scene in 2011, winning gold in the 200m Individual Medley at the ASA National Championships to secure a place at the World Championships in Shanghai.

Siobhan booked her place as the youngest swimmer on the London 2012 Olympic team with 100m Breaststroke gold at the 2012 British ASA National Championships. In 2014, she won her first British titles over 200m Freestyle and 200m Individual Medley, then won six medals on her Commonwealth Games debut for England at Glasgow 2014.

In 2015 Siobhan qualified for her third World Championships in Kazan, Russia, where she was part of a relay quartet winning the inaugural mixed 4x100m Medley relay and taking bronze in the 200m Individual Medley. 2016 also started well as she secured three titles at the British Championships in Glasgow including her favoured event, the 200m Individual Medley.

At the 2016 Rio Olympics, Siobhan nearly caused one of the biggest upsets in the pool as she delivered an outstanding swim in the 200m Individual Medley, almost beating Hungary's Katinka Hosszu to the title; she set a new British record of 2:06.88 in the process. She also achieved a finals spot and seventh place finish in the Women's 4x100m Medley relay, and a ninth place with the 4x200m Freestyle quartet. Her success continued the following year with three medals at the British Swimming Championships before a successful defence of her 200m Individual Medley title at her second Commonwealth Games, as well as further bronze medals in the Women's Freestyle relays.

The Glasgow 2018 European Championships served up a busy schedule for Siobhan, with four events and one medal - she claimed bronze as part of the Women's 4x100m Medley relay.

GEORGE OLLIS – TOWN CRIER
1881 - 1951

A painting of George Ollis by Keynsham artist Claude Gilliard

George Ollis, third from left, in 1931 at the Town Criers' competition in Lyme Regis, where he lost out to the local town crier

The tradition of town criers goes back many centuries, when they provided the main means of communication to townsfolk. As, at times, their messages conveyed bad news, (such as tax increases) they were protected by law, giving us the phrase "don't shoot the messenger".

In Keynsham, George Nicholas Ollis filled the role for thirty-one years until the formation of Keynsham Urban District Council in 1938. As Town Crier, he was very successful in representing Keynsham and won competitions on a number of occasions. In 1926, he won a special prize for best-dressed crier in the National Town Criers' competition held at Pewsey. His costume at the time was green, with knee breeches, buckled shoes, a three-cornered hat and powdered wig.

George Ollis worked for the Great Western Railway for many years and his success as town crier was reported in their in-house magazine in November 1926. He resigned when the UDC was formed and although the new administration asked him to continue his services, he felt unable to do so. The Council recorded their appreciation of his services and allowed him to retain his clothes of office, but stated he must return his bell to the Council. He died on 17 June 1951, aged seventy.

ELIZABETH FILKIN (NÉE TOMPKINS)
B 1940

Many of those who are successful become household names as a result, but one person from Keynsham whose achievements are less conspicuous is Elizabeth Jill Filkin. She was born Elizabeth Tompkins on 24 November 1940, the daughter of Frances Trollope and John Tompkins, who lived at Greyholme in Charlton Park. Elizabeth went to Temple Street Infants School and Bath Hill Junior School before moving in 1951 to Clifton High School in Bristol for her secondary education.

In her employment, she initially had a variety of roles in community work before taking a law degree at Birmingham University in 1973 and then spending eight years at Liverpool University where she lectured in social studies. Ms Filkin then became chief executive of the National Association of Citizens' Advice Bureaux, followed by several senior public sector roles.

in February 1999, she took a high-profile role in becoming the second Parliamentary Commissioner for Standards. Her role was to oversee the Register of Members' Financial Interests and the Code of Conduct for MPs. She was relentless in her thoroughness and in the course of her three-year term she made many enemies in Parliament and in the senior ranks of the government. The outcome was that at the end of this term, she was not invited to reapply for a further period: many commentators thought this was unfair.

Afterwards, Ms Filkin moved on to take senior roles in a wide range of regulatory and public bodies together with several non-executive directorships.

2011 saw the news dominated by the 'phone-hacking scandal' in which it became clear that some Fleet Street newspapers had accessed

messages on the mobile phones of victims of crime as well as many celebrities. This led to the closure of the *News of the World* and the setting up of several inquiries. One of these, set up by the Home Secretary, was led by Elizabeth Filkin, to recommend changes to links between the police and the media, including how to extend transparency; it reported the following January.

In the 2014 Queen's Birthday Honours Elizabeth Filkin was appointed Commander of the Order of the British Empire for 'public service'. At the time of writing, she continues to serve as chairman or director of several organizations in both the public and private sectors.

MARCUS TRESCOTHICK
B 1975

The man who some would claim as one of Somerset's greatest cricketers, alongside Gimblett, Richards and Botham, was born in Keynsham on 25 December 1975, a Christmas present for parents Lynda and Martyn. Dad was good enough to be offered a second XI contract with the County Cricket Club (which he turned down) and Mum was a traditional tea provider. Living in Oldland Common, Marcus Edward Trescothick was educated at Saint Anne's Primary School, followed by Sir Bernard Lovell Comprehensive, but

Marcus Trescothick (right) with Somerset colleague Andy Caddick

he learned his cricket at Keynsham, where his father was a stalwart of the Cricket Club.

By his own admission, his 'interest in schoolwork may have been minimal', but he was a notable schoolboy cricketer and footballer. He burst onto the national cricket scene in June 1987, aged eleven, scoring 183 not out for Avon Schools' Under-11s team, attracting the attention of local BBC television and the *Bristol Evening Post*. After two games for Gloucestershire Under-11s, Somerset realised he was one of theirs and signed him up.

His first century in senior cricket was for Keynsham in 1989 and one year later he was in the England Under-14s, with Andrew Flintoff. He first played for Somerset First XI on 12 May 1993. By the year 2000 he was playing for the full England side and went on to score 5,825 runs in Test Matches for his country, with fourteen centuries, until 2006, when the onset of depressive illness made it impossible for him to travel abroad, away from his family. This did not stop him from playing for Somerset, and his County career continued, with his taking the captaincy from 2010 to 2016. The following year he broke the record for the most first- class centuries scored for the County. He retired from professional cricket in 2019, his last appearance at Taunton being on 26 September; he was greeted with a standing ovation and left the field with a guard of honour formed by the opposing Essex team.

JUDD TRUMP
B 1989

Judd Trump was born in Whitchurch, Bristol on 20 August 1989. He started playing snooker aged three years when his father gave him a mini-snooker table and he showed talent from that day on, progressing over the years to become one of England's greatest snooker players.

At the age of five Judd was registered with Knowle Snooker City where his talent was recognized. Then, aged seven, he joined Keynsham Snooker Club at the Leisure Centre complex. Here, he made his name by being a regular weekend tournament winner - which sometimes involved competing against fifty competitors much older than himself. A year later he gained a sponsorship to help with travelling expenses as he was entering competitions away from this area.

At the 2014 German Masters Tournament   Photo Martin Rulsch, Wikimedia Commons

Judd won the Under-13 years English Championship; at ten years old he became the Under-15 Champion and, aged fourteen, still at Hartcliffe School where he was greatly admired, he became the youngest player to make his first competitive break of 147, beating the record set by Ronnie Sullivan in 1991.

In 2005, Judd turned professional and he was only the third seventeen-year-old to qualify for the World Championship at the Crucible in Sheffield. He has had a remarkable career over the years since then with highlights such as 2011, when he won the China Open and the UK Championships. A year later he was the first winner of the International Championship held in China and held the top spot in the World Rankings for several weeks. He won the Australian Open in 2014 and in 2015 he became champion of the first World Grand Prix. Following a slight dip in form, 2019 was a very successful year for Judd: on 20 January he won the Masters, defeating Ronnie O'Sullivan 10-4 in the final, and four months later took his first World Championship title in Sheffield, beating John Higgins 18-9 in the final. Three more titles before the end of the year took him to No 2 in the world at the close of 2019.

Judd is said to be a quiet, unassuming man who has made his family and many friends proud of all he has achieved. His brother, Jack, now works with him and he practises regularly in Romford, Essex, where several of the top snooker players are based.

CHRISTOPHER WIGGINS
1917 – 2002

Chris was a member of a well-known family building firm in Keynsham which had been established by his grandfather Edward Wiggins. His father, also an Edward, died when Chris was fifteen but he, his mother and a manager continued to run the business.

Chris was born in 48 High Street in 1917 and was the eldest of four children. He was educated at Bristol Grammar School and, after studying at technical college, became a junior surveyor in Devizes and Melksham before receiving his call-up papers in 1941. He joined the Royal Artillery and was sent to Singapore just before it fell to the Japanese. The story of his three years as a Prisoner of War, spent mainly in Korea, is detailed elsewhere. Although there were many unpleasant experiences, Chris was always at pains to say that he was not treated as harshly as Japanese PoWs in some other theatres.

When the war ended in 1945 Chris was in the northern part of Korea and the camp was liberated by the Russians. He eventually arrived back in England on the Queen Mary on 15 November, surprised to see thousands of people on the quayside, with bands, assembled to welcome the troops home.

Back in Keynsham Chris became involved with the family business and over the years played a major role in the life of the town. He had played for Keynsham Rugby Club until he joined the Army; on his return he rejoined and worked hard to raise the reputation of the Club. He was secretary for many years and was awarded life membership for his outstanding service.

Chris was a good-hearted man and he was concerned for the welfare of others, particularly the elderly and infirm. This led him to join the Keynsham Rotary Club and he also become involved with the League of Friends of Keynsham Hospital. As a Rotarian he organized many community events such as summer outings, Christmas shopping trips and visits to concerts. Chris took his turn as President of the Rotary Club in 1962 and eventually completed 47 years' service to the Club.

His work for the Hospital endeared him to staff and patients, even to those in the High Street who responded to his collecting box on the Hospital Flag Day! Chris not only 'did the rounds' of the Hospital faithfully week after week, chatting to the patients and giving them encouragement and affection, but also organized the annual Hospital Fête which raised thousands of pounds for the improvement of patients comfort and welfare.

A man of many interests, he was also an enthusiastic member of the Keynsham & Saltford Local History Society, doing considerable research into many aspects of the town's past as well as his own family tree.

CHAPTER 2
THE CHANGING FACE OF KEYNSHAM SHOPS

The shops along the High Street and Temple Street have been at the heart of Keynsham life for several hundred years. It is impossible here to chronicle the many occupiers and new buildings on each site, but since 1945 there have been enormous changes in retailing and in society that can be illustrated by looking at a sample of businesses and premises. In this chapter we move from the junction with Station Road, by the Parish Church, to the top of Bath Hill and Temple Street, and then look at the more recent retailing scene.

NO 1 HIGH STREET

Next to the Church, No 1 High Street, occupied at the time of writing by Davies & Way estate agents, is typical of many in the High Street which have undergone a change of use over the last 200 years, with the general building shape remaining the same but the glass frontage becoming more of a feature and the signage becoming more prominent. This building was originally one of the many public houses in the High Street: in 1841 it was called the Black Horse, then the Railway Tavern, until this closed in 1956, when the photograph was taken. It then became the South Western Electricity Board (SWEB) showroom until, after a succession of short-term occupants, it was taken by Davies & Way. The adjoining property is occupied, in 2020, by California Nails, one of several beauty businesses.

THE CO-OP

In 1945, many of the shops in the High Street, Bath Hill and Temple Street were individually owned and run by local persons. Chappell Brothers in the High Street and Grimes in Temple Street were two prominent grocers who realized the importance of retaining business; they provided their customers with a personal service; you could place an order in person, then collect later or have the goods delivered to your home; not too dissimilar from the online delivery service of today. But competition was on its way, in the form of the Co-operative Society, which brought a new approach to retailing.

The Co-operative movement originated in the north of England in 1844. In 1863, independent Co-op societies set up the Co-operative Wholesale Society (CWS), to supply the various societies with a range of products – the country's first chain store operation across more than one type of product. In Keynsham, perhaps surprisingly, the local Co-operative Society started in 1894, serving only its forty members in what was nothing more than a village. It was too small to survive and in 1905

merged with the much larger Bedminster Co-operative Society, which in turn was swallowed up by the Bristol Society. Their first shop was opened by 1911 opposite the Church and by 1915 the attraction of the 'divvie', a share of the profits paid to all member customers, had become established and the Keynsham shop moved to larger premises at No 25-27 High Street, next to the then-Foresters Arms: this remained the principal Co-op grocery shop in the town.

As part of a larger organization, the Co-op provided serious competition for the town's established grocers, introducing new ideas, selling a wide range of groceries, including meats and dairy produce, at a good price; customers could even select some of the goods for themselves – self-service had arrived. The Co-op also provided a home delivery service for bread, milk, groceries and meats; another initiative enabled purchasing using prepaid tokens instead of cash. Before long the Keynsham operation had expanded beyond food; by 1930 the Co-op had established several

A rare view inside the Grocery Shop at 25/27 High Street in 1954

stores in the High Street. At No 29 (Timbercraft in 2020) they opened a shoe shop. On the opposite side of the road next to the Victoria Methodist Church, they had double-fronted premises occupied variously by furniture, general homeware and menswear sections, which were in direct competition with the nearby traders. This shop, illustrated (above, top left), closed about 1965, to be replaced by Whiting's furniture store.

Another of the Co-op's High Street outlets in Keynsham was the drapery store at No 46, seen in the photograph (above, lower left) in 1963, with the newly opened Post Office beyond. This building was later demolished, to be replaced by the block that in 2020 is home to Shoezone and Barclays Bank.

Only one Co-op property has survived into the 21st century: No 24 High Street, which started post-war as a modern food store and after a period as a Freezer Food Centre was converted to a funeral parlour in 1998. It remains in this use in 2020 – the last survivor of a chain that once had a major presence on the High Street.

The Former Grocery Shop in 2020

WOOLWORTHS

Woolworths in 1955

The Woolworths site as TSB in 1991

The idea that a 'high street' should consist of nothing but shops and similar businesses such as banks is a post-war concept that has developed from the planning control imposed by local authorities. Until the 1930s, Keynsham High Street contained a mixture of shops, banks, houses, public houses, a garage and a factory. An example of residential use was numbers 13 and 15, originally two cottages, later combined into a single house.

One of the chain-stores that expanded throughout the United Kingdom during the 1960s was FW Woolworths; its first branch in Britain opened in Liverpool in 1909. In 1955, Woolworths reached Keynsham; following the demolition of number 13-15, they built a new store (later replaced by a branch of TSB Bank). This was known for giving good value and became popular in particular for its pick and mix sweets, Chad Valley toys, Ladybird children's clothing and small household accessories. Many teenagers in the 1960s bought their records there and Woolworths had a mix of lines unlike that of any other chain.

Throughout the 1980s, competition from the larger supermarkets, which increasingly stocked non-food lines, and other specialist stores such as the DIY chains, put pressure on Woolworths. Profits fell, many larger stores were reduced in size and smaller ones closed. The Keynsham premises closed in 1989, leaving High Street shoppers no longer able to experience the "wonder of Woolies".

HALL'S NEWSAGENT

The newsagent, or 'paper shop', has been a fixture on the British high street since the nineteenth century. Of course, it was never just a place for buying newspapers and magazines, but also a tobacconist and sweetshop.

Rosewell Hall's shop at No 51 High Street gave employment delivering papers to many schoolboys over the years but was just one of several such businesses in the town centre. On Station Road stood Russell Harvey's, whilst near the top of Bath Hill, three generations of the Church family ran a very successful business from about 1935 and, across the road, Ogborn's sold newspapers as well as stationery, toys and art materials from before 1960 until their closure in 1991. Other competitors, such

as Kiosks, lasted less time.

In the early 1960s, Mr Hall moved a few doors along the High Street to No 43, as the premises shown in the photograph were demolished to be replaced by new shops now occupied by Dorothy House and Ladbrokes.

In early 2020, the centre of Keynsham supports only one newsagent, Church's, and this appears likely to close. The habit of buying newspapers has declined, with the circulation of the main local paper, the *Bristol Post* (formerly *Evening Post*) falling from a peak of almost 200,000 in the 1970s to about 11,000 in 2020. Similarly, the proportion of adults who smoke has fallen by about two thirds since the 1950s. Combined with the selling of newspapers by supermarkets, the resulting loss of business, mitigated in some cases by sales of National Lottery tickets since 1994, has made it impossible for these traditional shops to continue.

STRUDWICK'S

The history of Strudwick's is as much about the changing role of buildings on the High Street as it is about the shop itself.

Number 53 was built in about 1804 as a Wesleyan chapel. This building is typical of many properties where, despite changing use, the historical design has survived. The general shape is as built, although an additional storey was added later. Hidden by the signboard in the photograph, the late Georgian arched doorway remains; the positioning and number of windows are original, although the multi-paned arched windows have gone.

By 1887, the chapel congregation had moved to the new Victoria Methodist Church and the premises were sold; they first became the offices of the Persian Gulf Ochre Company who owned the Colour Mill in the park and then underwent a period of industrial use. More than twenty people were employed there in the Throsper factory in the manufacture of boot eyelets, using local brass, and later reputedly for producing corsets.

In 1936 the building was taken over by Ivan Strudwick, initially as an ironmonger's. Later

Strudwick's in the 1950s

he developed it into an electrical store and in the early 1950s the young people of Keynsham would sit on the remains of the wall in front and stare in wonder at the small black and white soundless flickering television displayed in the window.

Strudwick's closed in 1983 and the Halifax Building Society, later Bank, bought the building. The frontage has been refurbished: the ornamental bargeboards have gone, but the original doorway has been revealed. Of all the

buildings on Keynsham High Street, No 53 is perhaps the most imposing and it has certainly had the most varied history.

EDWARD JOLL

It would have been inconceivable to the first Mr Edward Joll, when he started his Gentleman's Outfitters business in Bristol in the nineteenth century, that a hundred or so years later there would be no demand for such a business on a typical British high street.

In 1933 Edward Joll II, who had taken over the family business in Bristol, moved to Keynsham. Number 55 High Street, immediately to the right of what is the Halifax premises in 2020, was originally a private dwelling house until, in 1896, it became Newport Bros, Gents' Outfitters. Mr Joll took over the premises to carry on what would be over one hundred years of the family business; it continued when Edward Joll III took over from his father in 1966 and he remained trading until 2004.

From 2005, his former premises have been occupied by a tanning and beauty salon, typifying the move away from retail outlets.

For about thirty years after the end of the Second World War, every high street supported one or two men's outfitters. Although dress was steadily becoming more casual, there was sufficient demand for suits and other formal wear from office workers and for special occasions. As well as Edward Joll, Keynsham tailor and outfitter Percy Baker ran his shop at 28 High Street, close to the Fear Hall, from 1945 until about 1975.

The individual businesses run by Messrs Joll and Baker prided themselves on their standard of tailoring and the bespoke service they provided. Everything was made-to-measure. As well as suffering from the fall in demand for formal clothing, they could not compete with the lower prices offered by the department stores and national chains with off-the-peg clothes manufactured in bulk, first in Britain and later abroad. Fosters menswear took a corner site at the bottom of Rock Road in the 1960s and there was also a branch of Hodges, a Wales-based chain, at 52 High Street, now occupied by a travel agent. After these closed there was a long period – until the opening of Suave Owl in 2017 – when there was nowhere in Keynsham where one could buy a man's suit or tie.

THE NATIONAL CHAINS

Until the 1950s, the shops in Keynsham High Street, in common with local high streets across the country, were almost all owned and run by local people, some of whom had traded for several generations. As we have seen, the only significant exception was the Co-op. Local retailers enabled residents to buy from a range of grocers, furniture and clothes shops; indeed all the essentials of life could be found without leaving the town.

A bus-ride away, the centres of Bath and Bristol had many national department stores and other chains but other than the banks and Boots the Chemists, Keynsham did not – presumably it was too small to generate enough custom. New building increased the population rapidly in the 1950s and 60s and the national chains gradually established a presence. Woolworths were one of the first, arriving in 1955, as described previously, and they were followed in the 1960s by Halfords, Currys and Lloyds Chemists. Later, FADS provided home decorating products, taking over a business originally run by Doreen Wiltshire from 1949 to 1964 but later taken over by a Bristol firm. Among the smaller outlets were John Menzies, Dewhurst butchers, and Brooks the cleaners.

In 1967 there was concern over the number of vacant shops in the town centre but overall, business was good. New outlets arrived as building societies and estate agents expanded. However, by the mid-1980s the retail boom for small high streets was really over. Keynsham's proximity to the fringe of Bristol meant its shoppers were especially vulnerable to the lure of the out-of-town retail parks with their

easy access and car-parking. The retail chains opened larger premises at these sites, resulting in Halfords closing in Keynsham in April 1994 and FADS moving to Brislington at the end of the same year. Some fashion stores have survived but most of these chain retailers have gone forever.

THE SUPERMARKETS ARRIVE

The corner unit of the Town Hall development, seen in the early 1970s

Post-war Keynsham saw numerous changes to the commercial properties in the High Street/Temple Street/Bath Hill area, with many of the two hundred-year-old buildings starting to make way for 1960s 'development'. In 1960, major works started with demolition around Bath Hill to make way for a new shopping complex, along with the new Town Hall, library and a clock tower. Some ten years later the housing and shops further along Temple Street were also being demolished to make way for the eventual construction of a new fire station, office block, leisure centre and housing. This combined re-development had a major effect on the provision of shops in the town.

By 1966, the new Town Hall and library were complete and most of the shop units were taken; amongst them was the larger corner unit which was occupied by a supermarket called Victor Value (with their VV logo), a budget, low-end grocery company based in London. This marked the entry of the modern supermarket into Keynsham; it would have a big impact on customer shopping habits and increase competition for the traditional local traders. Shopping trolleys were now in use and customers started saving 'pink stamps' to use for future purchases. But in 1968, the company was bought by one of the future major players in the retail trade, Tesco, and the Keynsham store was soon re-branded.

The area at the bottom of Rock Road and the top of Bath Hill became a focus for competing supermarkets over the next twenty years. When Tesco decided to concentrate on larger stores their corner plot was taken over by Kwik Save whilst across the road, the corner site, which had been a grocer's since at least 1900, when it was occupied by Cridlands and later Grimes, was redeveloped for Gateway Stores, who subsequently took over both the nearby Key Markets and Fine Fare further away;

Grimes' shop at the bottom of Rock Road, seen in the mid-1960s

The site as redeveloped by Gateway

in 2020 the site is occupied by Iceland.

As well as the larger units taken by supermarkets and national chains, many more small shops became available. First were those along the frontage leading to the Library and on Temple Street; 1976 saw further units completed beneath the Riverside office complex and near the Leisure Centre. Retail was booming at this time and tenants for the new shops were found readily.

The Co-operative Store at Broadmead, opened in 1990

During the 1980s the major supermarket chains grew steadily, by opening superstores too large to be sited in most town centres. Tesco opened such a store in Brislington in 1985; this attracted customers from Keynsham, as did Asda at Longwell Green. Business at Keynsham's small supermarkets declined and several closed. In 1989, the Co-op obtained permission to build a superstore at Broadmead on the edge of the town. This opened in August 1991 but, with a floor area of 27,000 sq ft, it was only medium-sized by superstore standards.

Despite various upgrades and re-brandings – it was known as Leo's initially – the store was never profitable and the site was sold to Waitrose, who opened in March 2014. With a combination of more expensive lines and the ability to draw in customers from a larger area the new owners have succeeded in making a success of the operation, although its location makes it difficult to reach for residents in parts of Keynsham, reducing its impact on the town centre.

THE AGE OF THE COFFEE SHOP

Plans to develop a modern supermarket in the centre of Keynsham were first mooted in 1984 but did not come to fruition until Tesco returned to the town with a 20,000 sq ft development at St John's Court. This opened in October 2010, with the advantage of a car park accessible from both Charlton Road and Bristol Road, upgrading what had been an unsurfaced parking area for many years.

By that time the world of shopping had changed completely from the immediate post-war era. Keynsham shoppers now expected to do most of their food shopping at one shop and the great majority wanted to park their car outside that shop. The Tesco meant that they could do that within town, but it left the High

Street with only Banable's as a butcher and Buss's as a greengrocer. Demand for bakers has continued, with regional and national chains such as Parsons and Greggs providing both bread and fast food.

In 2020, the High Street has a wide range of businesses, but many are not traditional retail, with travel agents, estate agents and opticians for example, providing work and essential services – but these are not shops that one visits many times in a year. Inevitably, this makes the shopping streets less busy. On the other hand there has been growth in charity shops. The first of these was Oxfam, which arrived at the beginning of the 1980s, but by 2020 there were seven with some offering a wider range of products, such as new furniture.

Recent building work, such as the Civic Centre and Temple Street re-development, continues to incorporate retail space; although lettings take some time, new tenants are being found. There are some specialist shops, which trade partly on-line, and a slowly increasing number of restaurants and coffee shops. Coffee One opened in 2010 and has been followed by the Bonzo Lounge, Costa Coffee and several smaller establishments. As demand for traditional shops declines, the growing local population enables these new enterprises to succeed.

Finally, a reminder of one of the town's family businesses that was a favourite with gardeners and children buying pet food for many years:

One of Keynsham's last family-run shops was Nix's Garden Shop, shown with the family in 1993

CHAPTER 3
EDUCATION AND HEALTH

M odern life relies on a range of services provided at public expense by a variety of agencies, both national and local. In this section we look at aspects of just two, relating to education and healthcare, considering their origins and how they have developed to give the arrangements we have today.

PRIMARY SCHOOLS IN KEYNSHAM

Keynsham's first primary school in the modern sense opened on Bath Hill in 1857. It was known as the Keynsham Parochial School and, in 1863, the log shows that there were 71 children and three staff on the roll. These numbers fluctuated depending on illnesses and demands made by parents for help in potato planting or apple picking for example. Parents were expected to pay one penny a week per pupil but some large

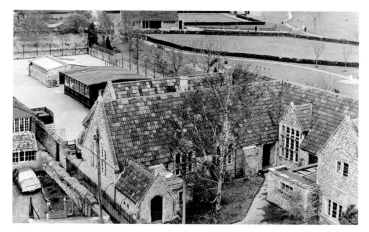

Bath Hill, the Junior site of Temple Primary School, about 1970

families found this difficult, which meant those children missed out on their education several times a year. The Infant School was created as a separate entity in 1864 but remained in the Bath Hill building until October 1894 when it moved to its own premises on Temple Street. By 1938 the number of pupils on the combined registers was 204, and it increased further during the war. In 1968 the two schools were merged – although still on two sites - and the name changed to become Temple County Primary School. Over the years other schools opened in the town, so the number of pupils fell to only 80 in 1960, although at the time of closure in 2007, this had risen to 167.

All the other primary schools in Keynsham were constructed after the Second World War in response to the growth in the population of the town. Keynsham County Primary School was the first of these, built at Kelston Road in the early 1950s to serve the newly-built estates on the south side of the town.

On the other side of Keynsham, most of the Chandag estate was built between 1955 and 1965. Chandag Junior School and Chandag Infant School were constructed, effectively on the same campus as Wellsway, first as a combined primary, with the Infant School getting its own building in 1966. They are still (2020) run as separate establishments although both are now part of the Wellsway Multi-Academy Trust.

St John's Church of England School opened in Charlton Park in September 1960, with a formal ceremony by the Bishop of Bath & Wells on 13 June 1961; a number of pupils and staff moved from Temple County Primary. The school educates about 200 children from four to eleven years of age. In September 2015 it became part of the Wellsway Multi-Academy Trust.

The school choir at the opening ceremony of Saltford Primary School

As part of a reorganization of primary education in Keynsham in September 2007, Temple Primary and Keynsham Primary merged to form St Keyna Primary School. This ran in the three existing school buildings until pupils and staff finally moved into the new building at Monmouth Road in June 2008. The old County Primary building at Kelston Road was then demolished; the Victorian buildings on Bath Hill and Temple Street were subsequently redeveloped as housing.

To the south of the town centre lies Castle School in Newlands Road, a community school that opened in 1968. New housing nearby has funded the expansion of this with four new classrooms and a hall opened in 2018 to double capacity to 420 pupils. As a result of housing development at the former chocolate factory, September 2017 saw the opening of Keynsham's newest school: Somerdale Educate Together Primary offers thirty reception class places each September and includes pre-school provision. Being a new establishment, this became the first 'free' school in Keynsham and the innovative building provides a splash of colour, contrasting with the brick of the refurbished factory buildings.

SALTFORD PRIMARY SCHOOL

The old school building in the High Street was built in 1874 and enlarged in 1910. During the Second World War it accommodated evacuee children who had come from London. Following the 1944 Education Act, the school became a voluntary controlled Church of England School. After the war, the population of the village increased: men and women returned from the forces, many living with their parents until new homes were built. The number of young families grew and the village school could not accommodate them, so in 1953, the infants were moved to Ellsbridge House on the A4 road near Keynsham as a temporary measure. This had been a large family house belonging to John Simmons and his family. It had large ground-floor rooms, a kitchen, covered areas for indoor play and a spacious garden. A coach picked up the children from the Memorial Park in Saltford at the end of Manor Road every morning, and returned them at the end of the school day to be met by their parents. This arrangement proved very successful and carried on until the new school in Claverton Road was opened in September 1961, when the children moved in from the old school and Ellsbridge House.

SECONDARY EDUCATION

Before 1935 there was no secondary education provision in Keynsham. Therefore, many pupils from Keynsham attended Bristol secondary schools, with the Somerset Education Committee paying £700 a year for them. This was in addition to the fees paid by parents. Other children attended private schools in Bath and Bristol. A growing view that education should be provided free of charge was resisted on the grounds that those who could not afford the charges were able to get assistance under then current legislation.

As a result of the lack of local school provision and the steady increase in the population of Keynsham, arising from the construction of the Fry's factory and the new paper mill, Somerset County Council decided in 1929 that a new school was required. Finding a suitable site and acquiring the land took time and construction was not completed for some six years: 'Keynsham Council Senior School' was finally opened on 26 June 1935. The School, in St Francis Road, had ten staff and 222 boys and girls aged between eleven and fourteen. Its catchment area was Keynsham Junior School, Compton Dando, Norton Malreward, Whitchurch and Saltford.

The provision of education in Keynsham and Saltford since 1945 reflects the efforts of governments to improve it. In 1944, the Butler Education Act was passed; this raised the school-leaving age to fifteen and planned to provide universal free, state-funded, secondary education in three types of school: grammar, secondary modern and technical. Local authorities were responsible for implementing this system but it took several years to plan and construct the necessary new schools.

As a consequence of the Act, Keynsham Grammar School opened in September 1956 for pupils who had succeeded in an Eleven Plus examination which was intended to select the top 25% for education up to the age of eighteen. Their numbers were further limited by the accommodation available and the requirement for small classes. The rest went to Wellsway County Secondary School – a secondary modern – which opened at the same time and

Broadlands School in about 1980   Photo courtesy of Skyviews

used the same building initially. These pupils left at fifteen. To prevent confusion, Broadlands Secondary Modern was given its present name at the same time.

Although the Butler Act envisaged technical schools, none were established in the Keynsham area. Some of the grammar schools existing before 1945 stayed in the fee-charging sector, alongside the 'public' and other private schools. Another form of selection operated from 1945 to 1976, with public funds paying for pupils at private 'Direct Grant' schools. Later, some Keynsham pupils benefitted from the Assisted

Ellsbridge House, Bath Road

In 1975 the Wellsway curriculum included allotment gardening

Places Scheme, which paid for pupils to attend private schools, until it ended in 1997.

The widespread introduction of comprehensive education after 1965, and the raising of the school leaving age to sixteen in 1972, together with increasing population, meant that our secondary schools expanded significantly. Broadlands took in its first comprehensive intake in September 1970 and the two senior schools on Chandag Road were combined to form Wellsway Comprehensive in the following year. At Broadlands, five new buildings were constructed between 1963 and the mid-1970s to cater for all abilities and the wider age range. At this time, part of the Crown Fields, off the old Bristol Road, was also acquired as a new playing field, with access via a new footbridge.

In the period since 1997, government changes have led to the introduction of self-governing, multi-academy trusts accountable to and funded by the Department of Education. As a result, Wellsway converted to an Academy in 2011, followed by Broadlands, which joined the Academies Enterprise Trust in December 2012. Both schools have continued to grow: at September 2019 Broadlands had 628 students aged eleven to sixteen on the roll while Wellsway had twice that, including the sixth form. In addition, the Wellsway site now includes the separately-managed IKB Academy, opened in 2015, a Studio School providing technical education to some 180 students aged between fourteen and eighteen.

'Freedom of choice' has meant that some secondary age children travel to schools in Bath, including St Gregory's Catholic School and other faith schools, whilst some sixth formers travel out of Keynsham to St Brendan's on the edge of Bristol.

ADULT EDUCATION

Starting in 1946, a range of adult education classes was provided by the County Council at the County Secondary School, under the name Keynsham Evening Institute. By 1957 these were being held also at Ellsbridge House, Bath Road, where they continued until the 1980s. The Institute was based at Ellsbridge and courses, both afternoon and evening, covered a variety of subjects including typing, shorthand, languages, carpentry, wood carving, car maintenance, cooking for single men, guitar-playing and singing. Students paid termly and in the early years the classes were inexpensive. As well as Broadlands, some classes were held at Wellsway.

Changes in funding meant that the charges increased later and this contributed to the demise of these local authority courses.

HEALTHCARE – GENERAL PRACTICES

In 2020, Keynsham has three National Health Service general practices. We look at how these started and have changed over the years.

There were doctors practising in Keynsham from the late eighteenth century onwards but the links to modern times start with the first mention of Dr Charles Harrison in 1889. We know that he was renting Tregare House, at 44 High Street, about 1901 and bought the property in 1904. At about the same time, Dr William Peach Taylor came to Keynsham, newly qualified, and lived and worked at Failand House, also in the High Street. In 1905, he set up the Station Road Surgery at No 2, Hanover House. This was almost half a century before the National Health Service was set up, so patients had to pay for their consultations.

In 1923 Dr Claude Harrison joined his father at the surgery in Tregare House.

Dr Peach Taylor had posts in Bristol and was Public Vaccinator for the Keynsham Union (Workhouse). He built up a substantial practice in Keynsham and travelled around the town on a bicycle as well as owning a car – a rare sight on the roads then. When he retired in 1938 – at the age of 75 – Dr Norman Gerrish bought Hanover House with the practice and, in 1947, took on a partner, Dr John Field. The population of Keynsham and Saltford was approaching 8,000, but it increased rapidly and Dr Geoffrey Herepath joined the practice as a third partner in 1953 – he would stay for 34 years.

At this time the provision of surgery/consulting room facilities usually depended on the initiative of the doctor and Keynsham's third practice was set up in the post-war period by Dr Vera Dowling, who converted empty shop premises at No 4 Wellsway, close to the New Inn, into a surgery and waiting room. She was the first woman medical practitioner in the area, and worked until 1964 when she sold the practice to Dr Christopher Bailey.

Tregare House, where the Doctors Harrison lived and practised, seen just before demolition in 1959

St Augustine's Surgery, Station Road, at closure in 2018

A fourth general practice was set up in Keynsham when, to cater for the new residents of the Coronation Avenue/Queens Road area, the Council offered Dr David Munro the use of a building on the corner of the Queens Road rank of shops. This practice and the one at Wellsway helped each other to cover holidays; they were not originally linked although eventually the Queens Road surgery closed and Dr Munro joined Dr Bailey's practice.

Saltford patients were served by Keynsham's

Dr Bailey's former premises at Wellsway, Keynsham

West View Surgery in Park Road, built in 2000

Station Road practice, which held surgeries in a room adjacent to the former Central Stores on the corner of Bath Road and Beech Road. When Dr Herepath joined, he and his wife moved to live at Beech Road so that a permanent surgery could be established at their house.

In 1962, Hanover House was compulsorily purchased to make way for the Keynsham by-pass, so the Station Road Practice moved a short distance to the ground floor of No 4 Station Road (St. Augustine's) and acquired its present name. A fourth partner joined the practice in 1970 but left to be replaced by Dr Tom Garrett. After the untimely death of Dr Gerrish in 1971, Dr Tony Fox joined the practice, which covered a huge area extending down to High Littleton. When Dr Field retired in 1977, he was replaced by Dr Jane Wyatt.

Several Keynsham doctors provided a service as Medical Officer to the Union/ Keynsham Hospital. Dr Claude Harrison took this role for many years and was followed by several others; Dr Fox and Dr Richards started an active programme of respite admissions and discharges.

Some of the doctors pursued their specialist interests: Dr Fox left West View in 1980 to practice homeopathy full-time, being replaced by Dr William House, and by 1993 Dr Garrett had become very involved in medical teaching, so he and Dr Wyatt moved to part-time work.

After Dr Claude Harrison retired, his practice was bought in 1954 by Dr Douglas Bennett and his wife; they took new premises at a former nursing home in West View Road and renamed the practice. Obstetrics specialist Dr James Ree joined and cared for pregnant mothers, supporting births at home and at Keynsham Hospital. A second consulting room was set up at Dr Ree's house in Hurn Lane, to serve the growing Chandag Estate. After his death, the West View practice built a new surgery in the 1980s at the end of Severn Way with two consulting rooms and other facilities.

By then the practice had 5,900 patients; Drs Richards and Nutt joined full time, while Dr Wendy Coe and Dr Alison Wheeler created a pioneering job-share. The old main surgery was no longer suitable for a modern practice, so in December 2000 they moved into new purpose-built premises in Park Road on the land behind the previous clinic's car park. Retirements and changes to the partners meant that, in 2019, the practice had four General Practice partners serving 7,200 patients at its two sites.

Dr Bailey practised at his Wellsway surgery until, in the 1970s, he accepted an offer to move to new ground-floor premises on the west side of Temple Street as part of a re-development scheme. This had much more space and he was joined by several partners.

Meanwhile, an emergency out-of-hours service had been set up to cover Keynsham and district, and many of the doctors took part in this. Guyan's (funeral directors) agreed to take the calls, and the doctors had radios in their cars and kit boxes to deal with emergencies. This service might be considered a forerunner of the paramedic service. Further support for hospital admissions and emergencies came with the building, in 1965, of the Ambulance Station on West View Road, which provided a base for four vehicles.

The period since 2000 has seen a steady expansion of health service provision through general practices. Together with the increase in population and longer lifespans this has required both more doctors and support staff. In 2014, the Temple Street practice moved to the new Keynsham Health Centre and early in 2018 St Augustine's moved to modern accommodation at Somerdale. Not everything has changed: when the latter practice first had a telephone its number was Keynsham 43; it has always kept the same number but this is now preceded by many other digits.

Most recently, in 2019, the three general practices have come together to form the Keynsham Primary Care Network, serving a total of 25,000 people. This is led by two clinical directors, Dr Charles Bleakley, from West View, and Dr Nick Woodward, a partner at St Augustine's; while the constituent practices remain independent, the Network is intended to improve care by giving them more opportunities to share specialist staff.

HEALTHCARE - DENTAL SERVICES

Before the National Health Service was set up in 1948 all adult dental care had to be paid for, so many people did not have a dentist. It has been estimated that, nationally, 75% of adults had none of their own teeth remaining. NHS dental care was initially free and demand was enormous. Charges were introduced for dentures in 1951 and for other treatments later.

A dental practice was opened in Charlton Road, Keynsham in 1939 by Albert Constance. This closed but, in 1948, George Ferguson opened a new practice offering NHS treatment, next door to the Charlton Cinema, and this is still operating. In 1960, another opened in Charlton Park; 1968 saw this developed into a full-time NHS practice by Fred and Hilary Smedley. Other practices opened in the High Street and later in Bath Hill and the Wellsway. When the Keynsham Health Centre was built in St Clements Road in 2009, the Childrens' Clinic was moved there from Park Road, and an NHS dental service was opened for adults,

The Park Road Clinic and Mobile Unit in 1961

run by the Parks Dental Practice who also had the practice at 58 Park Road. This practice was taken over by BUPA in 2020.

Since the 1960s, oral health has improved substantially and by 2019 there was considerable demand for cosmetic work, which is not provided by the National Health Service. At the date of writing there were six dental surgeries in Keynsham, including that at the Health Centre, and two in Saltford. Of these, three provided treatment on the NHS with the others treating private patients only.

THE SCHOOL DENTAL SERVICE

Since 1918, local authorities had a duty to provide dental care for primary age children and, in 1944, this was extended to cover children of all ages. In the Keynsham area this was provided from 1948 by the Somerset Local Health Authority. This account by Fred Smedley describes life in the local School Dental Service in the 1960s:

"In 1960, as a newly qualified graduate, I attended an interview to join the Somerset County School Dental Service. This was held in the Dental Clinic which was then located on the first floor of Hazelwood Day Nursery at the top of Rock Road, Keynsham.

"I considered the equipment to be so poor compared with that used at Bristol Dental Hospital, I had decided, prior to the interview, that I would not be accepting the post. However, the Chief Dental Officer Mr Quentin Davies took me to the window and pointed out the new clinic which was being built in Park Road. The dental wing had two surgeries with a recovery room in between, a dark room for processing X-rays and a store. This was to become my base for the next eight years, while to treat children in outlying village schools I would use a mobile dental caravan which was usually parked in the playground.

"My area extended from Keynsham, south west to Burrington village. At East Harptree the mobile clinic was parked in the car-park of the Waldegrave Arms.

"While there I heard of a previous school dental officer who used to visit the Somerset schools on his motorbike, carrying portable dental equipment in the sidecar.

"With boiling hot sun in the summer, and freezing cold in the winter when even the air-line froze as well as the water pipes, it was a problem to start work every day. I had been assured that all schools would have an electricity point and water tap to connect

Inside the Mobile Unit

to, but this was not the case, and I found it a great help to have a working knowledge of both electricity and plumbing. One school didn't even have an electricity point for their own use, and I had to connect into the fuseboard. We didn't have Health and Safety in those days.

"The children liked us being in their playground – we joined in their activities and gained their confidence. At least with my nurse Edna Birt, who was well known in Keynsham, I was able to provide treatment for many children who had not received any before, or not for many years. Mr Charles Amos and his nurse Sylvia already treated children at Keynsham Grammar and Secondary Modern schools, and also the villages to the east of the area surrounding Bath down to Radstock. At that time, there was a great shortage of dental officers so Charles was assigned to look after Radstock and I took on Frome.

"Happily, the dental health of children improved significantly during the 1960s largely due to the introduction of fluoride in tooth paste and better dental education. Parents were anxious that their children should not suffer from the same dental problems that they had."

CHAPTER 4
LOCAL SPORTS CLUBS

Our district has a sporting tradition that goes back to the beginning of the twentieth century; in some cases earlier. We look at the story of some of the main clubs: their origins and the key figures in their success. In early 2020, all are flourishing and provide exercise, recreation and, of course, competition for thousands of local residents.

SALTFORD GOLF CLUB

The course opened in 1904 when a group of Bristol-based businessmen and politicians seized the opportunity provided by improved transport facilities to lease from the Earl of Temple, at a rate of £325 per annum, the land the Club uses to-day.

An initial course was laid out and this was soon improved following extensive advice from Harry Vardon, one of the world's leading players in the early twentieth century. During the First World War, the course was used for agriculture to such an extent that only nine holes were playable for the first five years afterwards. The inter-war years were a constant battle and the Club's survival was largely due to the generosity of the members. During the Second World War, the clubhouse became the headquarters of the local Home Guard and posts were sunk into most of the fairways to prevent enemy aircraft landing.

Following the war, the Club devoted much energy to negotiating modest rental increases from new landlords the Duchy of Cornwall, who had purchased the land in 1941. A new Club Professional, Mr Leslie Mouland, was appointed in 1953. His brief was extensive with his contract requiring him to be 'Salesman, club repairer, teacher, and caddy maker....to obey all reasonable orders and directions given by the Committee or other Officers and be the

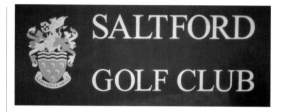

Greenkeeper'. His wage was £4 per week, plus accommodation. The annual subscriptions at about this time were six guineas [£6.30] for men and £4-14s-0d [£4.70] for ladies.

Mr Mouland became a wonderful asset to the Club and masterminded many improvements. When he arrived there was no electricity and no lavatory; he made the first significant changes to the course since it opened. In 1956, the West of England Championship was played at Saltford and it was won by Peter Allis. Through the 1950s and 60s improvements continued, with, for example, water being laid on at all the greens by 1958.

The Club expanded rapidly and developed a well-supported social side. In the 1990s, the course was given its modern layout with the introduction of new 2nd, 3rd, 7th, 10th and 17th holes and new greens at four others. The new clubhouse was built in 1984 and extended in 1991. The Club celebrated its centenary in 2004 and has played host to national, regional and county events.

KEYNSHAM BOWLING CLUB

Keynsham Bowling Club was founded in 1957. The previous year, a meeting had been called by Keynsham Urban District Council to discuss the possibility of forming a Bowls Club in the town to make use of the new facilities provided in the Memorial Park. It was decided that the charge for the use of the green would be one shilling [five pence] per hour, per player or 12 shillings per rink per match. Season tickets would be £2-10s [£2.50]. Although the green layout was excellent, due to financial restrictions it was not possible for the Council to provide any facilities that could be used as club headquarters or storage.

On 25 March 1957, the first general meeting of the Keynsham Bowling Club was held in the nearby Baptist Church. It was agreed that annual subscription for the Club should be 10s-6d [52½ pence] for ladies and gentlemen and 7s-6d [37½ pence] for pensioners. The first member of the Club was Mr R G Pope, a long-standing resident of Keynsham. Alderman Kenneth Brown was elected President, a post he held until the 1960s.

The new Club urgently needed some accommodation. Initially, a room at the back of the Lamb & Lark public house in the High Street was placed at the disposal of the Club to use as their Headquarters, courtesy of the landlord, Mr Beck. He also provided a Challenge Cup for competitions. Visiting teams and guests were entertained in the Drill Hall on Bath Hill. A building fund was soon launched for a club house and, after major contributions from some members, it was built by Messrs Moon and Co and opened on 4 October by Alderman Brown.

By the end of the first season, total membership had reached 58 and the Club had played 22 matches, winning twelve of them. From its foundation the Club was fully integrated for men and women - and was

probably ahead of its time in this. Membership continued to grow year by year. By 1962, the Club had acquired a very valuable collection of trophies donated by its members whilst others had made generous gifts of various items of equipment and furniture. Many of these trophies were still being competed for on the Club Finals Day in 2019.

The Club's success in membership brought with it accommodation problems and, in 1973, after a great fund-raising effort, a clubhouse extension was completed. As the Club progressed, the number of fixtures increased for both men and ladies, with some members gaining County honours. One important feature of Club activity was the introduction of a weekly 'Club Night' which is still very popular in 2019.

In 1981, the Club took over responsibility for the management of the bowling green from Wansdyke District Council and installed a water sprinkling system (which was upgraded

in 2019). Over the ensuing years, the green became recognised as one of the best playing surfaces in the area, leading to a number of prestigious events being held at the Club.

In 1992, due to an increasing membership, a further clubhouse extension was added (now the clubhouse beer store). This was initially financed by an interest-free loan of £20,000, but upon the death of his wife Lyn, John Coates, a longstanding member, took over personal responsibility for repayment of the outstanding amount. It is, therefore, no surprise that he features as a life member of the Club.

Over the ensuing few years, the Club continued to thrive with numerous successes at both individual and team level, particularly in the various Somerset county league and cup competitions.

In the late 1990s the Club suffered from some vandalism and the conifer hedge adjoining the tennis courts was largely destroyed by fire. It was replaced by the existing laurel hedge, which has enabled passers-by to see and appreciate the game of bowls.

The Club has relied on many individual members over the years, but mention should be made of John Mead, who took on the role of Greens' Manager in 1996 and was also elected Club President in 2003, celebrating fifty years' membership 2017.

In 2002, Les Hanson, a longstanding member who had served as Treasurer, Competitions Secretary and Triples Captain, resigned as he was moving to York. He was afforded life membership for his contribution over many years. Upon his death in 2012, the Club learned that Les had left a legacy to the Club of £5,000. His generosity enabled the Club to erect the canopy which stands at the front of the clubhouse today - 2020.

The Club continues to make a significant contribution at county level; one of the Club's life members, David Bendall, had the honour of being President of the Somerset Bowling Association in 2012 and he was followed in that same role in 2015 by the Club chairman Barrie Davis.

KEYNSHAM CRICKET CLUB

Keynsham Cricket Club in its current form was established in 1920. In 1927, the committee, led by chairman Frank Taylor, purchased land for the club on the Wellsway for £1,500, with a 5% mortgage secured by club trustee and local GP Claude Harrison. The ground was later named the Frank Taylor Memorial ground and has been the scene of many great matches.

Cricket continued at a modest level during the Second World War, although the facilities were shared in the summer with various cricketing regiments, numerous military parades and in the winter with sheep! In 1946 the Club, benefitting from an ever growing local population and returning servicemen, along with the opening of Broadlands School, provided sufficient players to develop two good teams with a first XI led by local GP Norman Gerrish, supported by core batsmen Doug Meredith, Ben Reynolds, Geoff Whittington and John Currie, and bowling led by Alan Heseltine and John Richards.

The ground facilities were basic but built with ingenuity typical of the time; the 'pavilion' was an ex-army hut purchased for £150 and the sight screens were made from surplus war metal. During the 1950s the ground, with its ever-improving facilities and wicket, started to host Somerset 2nd XI fixtures, along with player benefit matches, the first being for Yawar Saeed of Somerset and Pakistan in 1956.

Much later, in 2008, came the most notable

Testimonial Programme from 1982

benefit match, when the ground hosted a game as part of the benefit year for ex-Keynsham player Marcus Trescothick of Somerset and England. During the late 1960s his father, Martyn Trescothick, was part of an ever-improving Keynsham 1st XI led by Frank Phillips, that included local players Mike Beese, Roger Beese, and Nick Hillier. This team, strengthened by Bob Brooks, Graham Kendall, Trevor Brooks and Jim King would go on to win the Western League in 1979.

In one home match against Lansdown CC, Bob Brooks would become the unfortunate victim of a spectacular runout throw by a Lansdown fielder, a certain West Indian, Isaac Vivian Alexander Richards, who was gaining his residence qualification. But another ex-Wellsway pupil, off spinner Simon Butterfield, gained revenge by taking the wicket of Richards, who would go on to become one of the all-time cricket greats with Somerset and the West Indies.

Some of these players, such as Martyn Trescothick, Bob Brooks, Frank Phillips and Roger Beese were also founder members of the Keynsham Cricketers Football Club that played Somerset Senior League football at Manor Road playing fields. The club disbanded in 2015.

The 1980s would bring about changes on and off the field; Martyn Trescothick and Adrian Hillier were building a new team to challenge in the Western League, assisted greatly when another ex-Wellsway School pupil, left-handed batsman Richard Ollis junior, was available. Between 1981 and 1985 he played 37 first class matches for Somerset, scoring 1016 runs, his highest being 99 not out versus Gloucestershire.

Off the field, the wooden pavilion had become outdated and needed replacing, so in 1989 the project to replace it, led by local civil engineer Trevor Watts, started with the selling of club land near the Severn Way entrance for housing development to raise the necessary funds. In July 1990, the new pavilion was officially opened and, like the old one, features a clock face inscribed with the

The 1987 First XI in front of the old pavilion

name 'Sapper' Clarke, in recognition of his contribution to the Club during the 1940s.

Keynsham CC has always seen the importance of investing in youth, and has drawn new blood from the local schools, with Wellsway its primary source. One of the strengths of the Club has been the continued support of members through their contributions to the coaching or administrative side after they finish playing; the same family names have appeared over the years. Bob Dodds (1937-2000), former scorer, club chairman and president, typified this and the ground score-box has been named in his memory.

To generate sufficient income for grounds maintenance and other essentials, membership and sponsorship deals have been supplemented by an active social programme and hosting events such as a beer and cider festival. From 2017, Keynsham Hockey Club have been based at the Clubhouse, bringing in further income. In its centenary year, Keynsham Cricket Club

Marcus Trescothick and his father Martyn on Testimonial Day in 2008

fields three Senior XI teams, two Sunday XI teams, an occasional touring friendly XI, and three youth teams.

KEYNSHAM TOWN FOOTBALL CLUB

Winners of the Somerset Senior Cup in 1951-1952

The early years of football in Keynsham have been documented elsewhere, but during the latter part of the nineteenth and the early twentieth centuries, several teams were playing; among them Albert Road Villa, West End Rovers and several church teams. It appears that Keynsham Town was established in 1895; a report in the *Bristol Mercury* of 26 September 1898 states: "The Keynsham Football Club on Saturday played their first league match at Keynsham..." and by 1906 Keynsham AFC were competing in Division One of the Bristol & District League, in which they remained until relegated during the 1930s.

Various pitches provided a home in these early years, though some details are now a little unclear. First was 'The Hams', down towards the River Avon, until 1910, followed by the Gastons, where Gaston Avenue is today; then in 1925 Park Road, where they remained until moving to Charlton Road, just past St Ladoc Road, in 1930. There was also a spell at Manor Road playing fields, where the team had to change in a cowshed, on the land now occupied by the Rockhill park homes.

In 1939 the Club was disbanded for the period of the Second World War, reforming in 1945 and playing at the Crown Fields from 1947. The Club benefitted from the foresight of the then Committee, spearheaded by Roy Neal and Ken Dowling, in participating in the setting up of Keynsham Playing Fields Ltd, which bought the Crown Fields.

On the pitch, their fortunes improved and they took the Division Two title in 1949-50, earning promotion back to Division One. The Club won the Somerset Senior Cup in 1951-52, and again in 1957-58. In the late 1950s they joined the Bristol Premier Combination, before moving up to the Somerset County League in 1967.

In 1974, Keynsham joined the Western League. They finished second from bottom in 1975-76 and were relegated to the newly-formed Division One. In 1977-78 they became champions so returned to the Premier Division

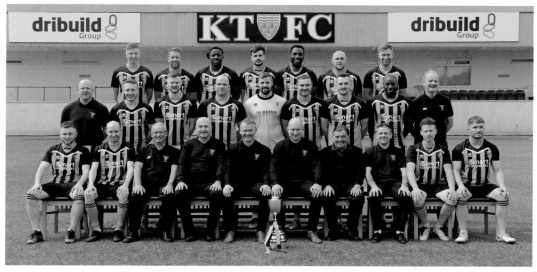

Winners of Division One in 2018-2019

until relegated once again at the end of the 1982-83 season. The Club then remained in Division One for fourteen years until promotion after being runners-up to Melksham Town under Graham Bird. The current president, Malcolm Trainer, was born very close to the ground and has many memories of his home club and great characters such as Ronnie Dicks, Barry Dundridge, Terry Hazel and the much-missed Terry Hooper. He recalls that football at the Club has been a rollercoaster ride with many sojourns in the Premier Western League over the years. After another dip in fortunes, the Club won the Somerset Senior Cup in 2002-03, but was relegated again in 2006-07 after finishing bottom of the Premier Division.

Over the years, team success has depended on the quality of many committed managers; from 2017 John Allen, formerly with Wells City, and Russell Holt managed the Western League side. John and his team achieved a creditable 'top four' position in his first season and, in 2019, secured a Premiership place, after finishing top of Division One by some margin. The team was doing well in their first season for many years at this level and were mid-table in March 2020 when the season was abandoned due to coronavirus restrictions.

Off the field, a new clubhouse was built in the 1970s, followed by new dressing rooms in 1984; floodlights were erected in 1989 with completion celebrated by playing Chelsea with Peter Bonetti leading their team. Later, the clubhouse was upgraded and seating added in the covered stand. Such improvements at the Club, formerly known as the Canaries but now simply as the Ks, have been dependent on having many volunteers, too numerous to list, working behind the scenes. In 2011, after Trustees secured a partnership with Brea-Avalon, managed by Barrie Newton, the stadium was renamed "The AJN Stadium" in memory of his son Alex. Over £1m was invested and the ground now boasts a modern synthetic surface, so it is used by many other clubs as well as the Ks.

Although it is the achievements of the first team that are generally recognized, in 2020, KTFC has FA Charter Standard Community Club accreditation for having made football available for all; it has over 400 juniors, a girls and ladies section, a special needs section and runs Keynsham Walking Football for the over-60s.

KEYNSHAM RUGBY CLUB

The First XV in 1971, with President Dennis Cockbaine

It is believed that a Rugby Football team existed in Keynsham during the 1890s, but not until 1923 was the Club formed with a group of players supported by a committee. The first matches were played at the 'Gastons' (the area that became Gaston Avenue) with post-match washing facilities consisting of four baths at the Lamb & Lark Hotel at a cost of £5 a season. The Chairman of the Club was Frank Taylor, also Chairman of Keynsham Cricket Club, while Dr Claud Harrison was elected as President in 1928 and continued until his death in 1957.

In 1930 the Club moved to Avon Road where the changing facility was a railway coach purchased for £14, including railway sleepers and delivery to Keynsham station. The coach was converted into a changing room with coal-fire heated showers. In 1937 the Club took the coach when it moved to Manor Road. Of the 56 playing club members in 1939, fifty went to war, of whom five were killed in action.

Post-War in 1945-46, the club returned to the 'Gastons' for one short season before moving to the Crown Field which was made possible by Mitch Bond and Jack Hickling who, with others, formed Keynsham Playing Fields Ltd. They leased out the pitches to both rugby and soccer clubs at an affordable rent. Changing rooms now consisted of an old adapted butcher's shop, with players washing in water tubs heated from coal-fuelled boilers. What happened to the railway coach?

Throughout the 1950s the Club was developing on the field with two strong teams through to a fourth XV in 1953. Dennis Cockbaine, former player and captain in 1947-48, was the driving force behind a plan to develop the youth players that would feed through to the senior level. For the first time, in 1961-62, the Club fielded a Colts XV; in the 1968-69 season Dave Whittington set a club record of 285 points and, in 1972-73, became the first ex-Colts player to captain the 1st XV.

The name of Dennis Cockbaine MBE became synonymous with the Club's post-war success. He was a player in the 1940s, then a dedicated committee member who became chairman from 1963 to 1970 and president from 1971 until his death in 2010. In the 1950-51 season he organized the most important match in the Club's history, against a star-studded International and County XV watched by 3,000

Celebrations in 2017 when the First XV won promotion at Chosen Hill, Gloucestershire

spectators: Keynsham lost the match, but the consolation was a profit of £65 which was used to fund a clubhouse extension and new showers. This was the start of a rebuild of the clubhouse, which was completed in April 1955 and included a bar – creating a new source of income for the club. Upon Dennis's death, one of the Club Trustees, John Hibbitt, was elected as president and continues to serve in 2020.

In the 1960s, the Club was helped by the emergence of young players from the new Wellsway schools, where rugby was now being taught by sports masters with a rugby playing background such as Bill Whistlecroft and Malcolm Lew. Malcolm Lloyd was one of the first pupils; after playing for England Schools teams he joined Bath Rugby, making 255 appearances as scrum half until his 'retirement' in 1976 after which he played for Keynsham. High quality school rugby coaching ran through the 1960s and 70s and in the 1970s-80s Wellsway School and the Club jointly hosted touring school sides from the twin town of Libourne. In 1967-68, Clive Buckle returned to the club as 1st XV captain and brought about much needed changes to cope with a demanding fixture list. He instigated a more professional structure and attitude towards coaching along with a change in the 1st XV shirt, with a distinctive plain yellow top replacing the traditional black and amber hoops.

In 1968, the Club purchased the land on which the pitches and clubhouse stood. This enabled, in the 1980s, construction of a purpose-built clubhouse with changing-rooms; these were sited above the level of the floods that regularly make the pitches fit only for seagulls. In 2007 the bottom fields – previously leased – were also bought, and this secured the Club's long-term future. Two of those pitches were enhanced by the installation of floodlights. Throughout the Club's history the social side has been a strong feature, with the Annual Dinner and notable guest speaker a highlight. As well as Club activities the grounds and buildings have been used for tent shows, firework displays and, in recent years, a Music & Cider festival, all bringing in valuable funds. The clubhouse itself is also used as a venue for weddings, conferences and dinners.

On the field of play, the club regularly fields four strong professionally-coached senior sides, with the 1st XV gaining promotion to the South West One West league in 2016-17. In addition (in 2020) there is a Colts XV, a Junior section and a highly successful mini-rugby section for the Under-12s, with up to 400 children participating on a Sunday morning.

KEYNSHAM AMATEUR SWIMMING CLUB

Keynsham Amateur Swimming Club (KASC) has come a long way as a competitive club, but no one really knows when it started. The Club existed before the Second World War and was restarted by Babs Rayner, with others, in the 1940s. When it was formally registered with the ASA (Amateur Swimming Association) in 1950, the Club was using the Beau Street Swimming Baths in central Bath. This was notable for its warm water, of a green pea-soup colour, which caused swimmers who dived to disappear from view. In 1961, Jean Findlay joined the coaching team as a poolside helper and went on to become a mainstay of the club for the rest of her life. She described these early years and said that in the 1960s the Club was a village affair, which taught all-comers to swim. Anyone who came paid sixpence into a little wooden bowl for an hour's teaching at any level.

At the Club's annual championships, support came from Bath Ladies Swimming Club, who "ran the event as correctly as the Olympics", giving out medals to add to the few cups the Club had at the time. One of the competitors knocked the turn-judge into the deep-end; when she was hauled out it was discovered that she couldn't swim!

The Keynsham Club then became more organized. Expertise was supplied by Anne Rayner, and in 1968 Helen Elkington, former coach to the Olympic Team, ran an ASA/Sports Council course for the Teacher's Certificate in Bath, which enabled coaches to become properly qualified.

In the early seventies, dreams of having a pool at Keynsham looked as though they would come true, and the organizers worked across Somerset to gain experience. Parents were trained to help and encouraged to gain an Instructor's Certificate. Next came the expansion of KASC, ready for the new six lane, 25m pool. A recruiting event was held at Chandag Junior School; it was a great success and the modern Club was born.

The new pool was booked every Wednesday evening, beginning by teaching across widths in half-hour sessions, with the few who wanted coaching getting an hour at the end of the evening. Soon, the group was divided into junior and senior squads and, with the help of new volunteers Angela and Michael Curry, the Club quickly had both squads at a good standard, and a synchronised swimming team as well.

From 1984 until the early 1990s the Club ran a water polo team. This soon progressed from a half-hour session on a Wednesday night across widths using two chairs as goalposts, to one-hour sessions with lengths and leading to an exhibition match between club members. The team went on to play and win the Bristol League, with several members also playing for the Somerset Team from Under-16s to Under-20s.

In recent times, competitive swimming has been supported and funded by many organizations and the KASC committee worked to obtain as much as possible for the benefit of club members. Proximity to the University of Bath gave opportunities for local swimmers to get the coaching and development that a local club could not offer. Whilst members still turned out for the Club in important galas and

Somerset Championships Squad 1999

competitions, they had the chance to be in the same team as the Great Britain Olympic Squad. When Jean Findlay wrote a history of the Club in 2001 she said that "it's only a matter of time before we will be cheering a KASC swimmer on the TV" and she was right; by 2012 Siobhan-Marie O'Connor was in the British Team in the London Olympics.

In 2000, the Club decided that it needed a Masters Squad, for the world of Over-25 competitive swimming, so this was set up on Wednesday evenings with coach Ulo Ruutel. The initiative was a success: in 2000-01 several competitions were entered, with 'Golds' going to several of the squad and many of them being picked for the Somerset Masters Squad.

Over the years KASC has won numerous County honours and trophies and, aside from the competitive successes, has helped many young people to learn to swim and enjoy the sport. The Club has always been entirely run by volunteers and after Lillian Bullard and Mike Ellaby retired, Lynne Bartlett and Thelia Beament took over as the principal coaches. Partnership with Bath University (now Team Bath AS) has continued, helping to develop swimmers who compete at county, regional, national and international level. When Hengrove 50-metre pool opened Keynsham became a network club to City of Bristol Aquatics. Kay Rex took over as Head Coach in 2019 and the Club continues to grow; in early 2020 it had over 180 members, with a total of some forty volunteers, including many former young swimmers who have become qualified coaches to pass on their expertise to the next generation.

CHAPTER 5
PLACES OF WORSHIP IN RECENT TIMES

For many centuries the only places of worship were the local Parish churches; attendance was compulsory and absentees were fined. However, by the late seventeenth century attitudes were becoming more enlightened and non-conformity started to spread in many guises. At first, gatherings were in private houses but as numbers grew, dedicated places of worship were created, especially in the nineteenth century. This is a brief history of all such buildings, concentrating on more recent developments.

ST JOHN THE BAPTIST CHURCH

The parish church of St. John's is the oldest building in Keynsham and its history is well documented. The churchyard, unused as a burial ground for over thirty years, was cleared of gravestones and levelled in 1958 to enable road widening. In the early 1970s Old Vicarage Green was built on the site of the old vicarage and the Bridges School, with a new vicarage being built to the rear of the church. Since then the Church has seen an extensive programme of restoration and re-decoration, with a major appeal from 1992 to 1997. In 2020, St John's celebrated the 750th anniversary of its foundation with a series of special events and it remains the venue for civic services and the town's Remembrance Sunday service.

ST FRANCIS' CHURCH

When the Park Estate was developed in the 1950s, two sites in Queens Road were allocated for churches. The Methodists took one but eventually the Anglican church was built on Warwick Road instead. A great fund-raising effort generated the £17,000 required for a building that would serve as both church and parish hall. On 23 August 1958 the new church was consecrated by the Bishop of Bath and Wells. Fittings and furnishings came from a variety of sources: the choir stalls were made from oak pews donated by Chewton Keynsham Church and St. John's donated candlesticks and an altar cross. In 1968, an unwanted pipe organ from a disused church in Midsomer Norton

was purchased for £50, with parishioners dismantling and re-erecting it themselves. Following more fund-raising, a new hall was built in 1987 and extended in 2016, leaving the original building as the actual church.

THE SOCIETY OF FRIENDS (QUAKERS)

Despite having a presence in Keynsham since the English Civil War, it wasn't until the twentieth century that the Quakers established a permanent meeting house in the town. In the mid-1930s Wallace Litten, a lifelong Quaker, came from Bristol to work at the Paper Mills. The group then slowly grew, meeting in various places in Keynsham but worshipping at Quakers Friars in Bristol, until a new study group was inaugurated in autumn 1954 in a house in Charlton Road. This was the real beginning of the Keynsham Meeting and on 1 July 1956 the first publicly advertised meeting for worship was held in the Church Room, Station Road. Various premises were then used until, in March 1957, the Friends took a seven-year lease of Milward House from the Bristol Co-operative Society, with the first meeting being held in July. At the 'Opening Gathering' on

Milward House, Bristol Road

14 November 1957 about seventy people were present – an unexpectedly large attendance. However, numbers eventually declined, and the Quakers left Milward House in 1988.

ST DUNSTAN'S ROMAN CATHOLIC CHURCH

St. Dunstan's Church, Bristol Road, opened in October 1935, much to the relief of local Catholics who had, up to that point, had great difficulty getting to Sunday morning Mass in either Knowle or Bath (there was no Sunday bus service then). With generous help from Downside Abbey, a church was built on the Bristol Road, surrounded by an old-world kitchen garden and fruit trees, including a huge mulberry tree. During the Second World War, the Catholic community was increased in size by a number of evacuee children from London, in the charge of four Sisters of Charity of St Vincent de Paul whose strange headgear at first caused some astonishment to people in the town. After the war, the size of the Catholic community continued to increase, and the garden and mulberry tree had to make way for a

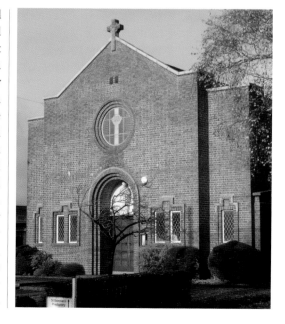

parish hall and car park.

In 2007, new statues of St Dunstan and Our Lady of Glastonbury were commissioned and an Allen Renaissance organ installed in the gallery. The American/Argentinian muralist Marcelo Lavalen painted a mural of the Tree of Life on the sanctuary wall for Easter 2009 and then, a second, depicting Christ in Majesty. Another improvement, in 2010, was an extensive refurbishment of the Parish Hall.

KEYNSHAM BAPTIST CHURCH

The earliest known reference to Baptists in Keynsham is a record of a preaching station in the town in 1715. In 1776, Protestant Dissenters of the Baptist Denomination registered a barn for religious worship in an orchard belonging to a Rev Mr Woolmer. This was sold in 1802 and the Baptists moved into their first building on the present site in the High Street; this included a burial ground – essential as dissenters often could not be buried in Parish cemeteries. However, the church was badly built and was pulled down in October 1834. Building of the replacement started immediately and the Keynsham Baptist Church on the High Street opened for worship, as the Ebenezer Chapel, on 21 April 1835.

Limitations on any development of the burial ground – the last recorded burial was in 1910 – have always frustrated plans to re-site the church. At the end of the 1960s much thought was given to moving onto one of the housing estates and, later, plans were drawn up for a new church and manse in Temple Street. Instead, between 1969 and 1976, the church was extensively modernised and improvements made to ancillary rooms and facilities. In 1988, further major rebuilding and alterations were made. The Church and its rooms have served many purposes – former pupils of Bath Hill School remember in the late 1940s being marched along Back Lane to the Baptist Rooms to have their daily lunch – and in 2020 continue to do so.

QUEENS ROAD METHODIST CHURCH

The 1950s saw the construction of the Park Estate and led to the creation of a flourishing Sunday School in the Zion Chapel situated at the junction of Temple Street and Albert Road. In time this proved to be too small and a new building was erected in Queens Road, opening for worship in 1958.

VICTORIA METHODIST CHURCH

There has been a strong Methodist presence in Keynsham ever since John Wesley first preached here in 1771 and by the 1851 census there was a Wesleyan Chapel, built in 1804 in the High Street (occupied in 2020 by the Halifax Bank). In the early 1880s, the congregation purchased land at the bottom of Charlton Road and on this site the Victoria Methodist Chapel was built and opened for worship in 1887; the walls and railings that originally enclosed the site were taken away in the mid-1930s, leaving an open forecourt. The Key Centre to the rear of the

Methodist procession in Charlton Road, 1986

church, built on the site of a Victorian 'Dame' school, was opened in July 1971.

ZION PRIMITIVE METHODIST CHAPEL

A Methodist Society was formed in Keynsham, attached to the Bath Primitive Methodist Circuit and a cottage was bought for worship in 1854. This was replaced by the Zion Primitive Methodist Chapel, also known as 'Billy Wiltshire's Chapel', built on the site of the old National Day and Sunday School at the junction of Temple Street and Albert Road in 1861, all the work being done by members of the congregation. The last service was held on the 15 May 1958 after which the congregation moved to the new Methodist church on Queens Road. The Zion Chapel was demolished on 1 October 1966, leaving a pleasant green space. Some of the beams from the old Chapel were used in the renovation work of Chew Cottages.

BETHESDA UNITED FREE METHODIST CHAPEL

The Bethesda Chapel was erected and opened for worship in Temple Street in 1860, founded by a breakaway group from the Wesleyan Chapel in the High Street. After more than a hundred years there, the congregation decided to join the new Methodist Church in Queens Road and the last service in Bethseda was held on 28 August 1966. The chapel was then used for six months by the Elim Pentecostal congregation. As the last ever sermon was about to be given, the old clock suddenly fell off the wall and shattered on the floor – time had run out for the old building! It was decided not to exhume the bodies buried in the tiny graveyard to the front of the building but, instead, to concrete over the graves and pave the area. The chapel building subsequently became Cashman's DIY store but after a while, strange happenings were reported by the staff. Initially a mirror was broken one night, thought to be just an accident, but then paint was spilled over the floor, to be

A view inside the chapel, about 1958

followed by smashed woodwork, torn wallpaper and nails thrown everywhere. The directors eventually had the building exorcised and the vandalism stopped, to the relief of the staff; the building is now the home of Simply Carpets. Some older residents might remember pupils from the nearby Infant School using the chapel as a dining hall in the late 1950s whilst waiting for St John's Primary School to be completed.

FAIRFIELD TERRACE CHAPEL

Fairfield Terrace had its own Mission Hall which opened in 1893. Previously privately owned, along with an adjoining cottage, it was purchased in 1936 by a group of evangelicals who, after joining the Fellowship of Independent Evangelical Churches, renamed it the Fairfield Gospel Hall. In 1956 the former Isolation Hospital site at Balmoral Road on the Park Estate was purchased and the church was relocated into an existing building there. The Gospel Hall, along with Fairfield Terrace and Woodbine Cottages, were demolished in 1967, the site now forming part of the Memorial Park.

The Mission Hall is on the right, with Woodbine Steps in the distance behind

ELIM PENTECOSTAL CHURCH

The present Elim Pentecostal Church in Balmoral Road was officially opened in 1967, ten years after a one-week evangelistic crusade in the town. Initial meetings were held in the Co-op Hall, Charlton Road until the Fellowship was able to purchase the old Zion Methodist Chapel on Temple Street for £1,000. In 1965 they moved to Balmoral Road where they combined with the Evangelical Church (see Fairfield on previous page) in a building originally built by the American Army as a field hospital in the mid-1940s, and began construction of a low level church in 1966, with meetings held in the interim in the old Bethesda Methodist Chapel in Temple Street. Construction of the present church building commenced in 1980 and was completed in 1985 with most of the work being carried out by church members. Further extensions and improvements were made in the early 2000s.

THE SALVATION ARMY

On 19 May 1923, the Corps was 'opened' by a Tent Campaign believed to have been held in Albert Road with the Divisional Commander and other senior officers leading meetings. The first open-air meeting was held on the Weighbridge (at the junction of Bath Hill and High Street) where Captain E Webster and Lieutenant J Janes were appointed as the first Commanding Officers. The flag had been presented by Mrs General Booth to Captain Webster in the Albert Hall in London on 28 May 1923 and on 30 July the first soldiers were enrolled. There was at that time no Hall, and meetings were held in the Primitive Methodist Chapel.

in 1926, a wooden building, used as a hospital ward in the First World War, was purchased from the Ministry of Defence and re-erected at the bottom of Rock Road as a hall. The Salvation Army did not attract much support in the town and the Corps was one

of the smallest in England, so in 1983 it was decided to close the Hall and put it up for sale, with the final meeting being held on 27 June 1983. The site was eventually bought by the St. John's Ambulance Brigade for use as a training hall and parking area for their ambulance. The building was demolished in 2016 and the site redeveloped for housing.

JEHOVAH'S WITNESSES

The Keynsham Congregation started in 1958 as an offshoot of the existing Hengrove Congregation and met at Milward House. By 1968 this proved to be too small and the Jehovah's Witnesses rented the Co-op Hall in Charlton Road. After a great deal of remedial work by the congregation this became home until it, too, could not accommodate the growing membership and in 1995 the congregation moved to a hall in Bishopsworth whilst a search for a new site was carried out. The former Magistrates' Court on Bath Hill East proved to be the ideal location and following demolition of the old buildings, including the cells, a new Kingdom Hall was built and opened for worship in August 1999.

ST MARY THE VIRGIN, SALTFORD

The parish church of St Mary the Virgin is situated in the middle of the village, next to Queen Square. The exact date of construction is not known but the lower part of the tower is believed to be late Anglo-Saxon. During the Civil War, extensive damage was caused by a party of Roundheads. Alterations and 'improvements' were made during the nineteenth century and the fine yew tree in the churchyard was planted on 23 January 1821. There have been no major changes since 1851 although electricity was installed in 1928 and the old 'box pews' were removed in 1934. More recently, removal of the plaster ceiling in the nave in 1974 revealed a fourteenth-century collar-beam roof. In 1975, a modern stained-glass window was installed in memory of Cecil Ewins, a former church organist and choirmaster.

SALTFORD COMMUNITY CHURCH

In 2004, the Saltford Community Church was constructed on Norman Road after the Saltford Evangelical Church was demolished. The original building had been erected in the late 1800s at the instigation of Mrs Mallinson; it was originally called the Working Men's Hall then renamed the Mission Hall before changing again to the Saltford Evangelical Church.

CHEWTON KEYNSHAM MISSION CHURCH

Built in Chewton Road and used as a school from the first part of the nineteenth century, the building became empty after the children were transferred to Compton Dando School at the turn of the century. It was bought for £150 by a Mr Bush who offered to let it to the Vicar of Keynsham for use as a mission church at a rent of 25 shillings (£1.25) a quarter. In 1936, he gave the building to the parish of Keynsham and it continues in use as a church, with services held twice a month.

CHAPTER 6
DEVELOPMENT AND TRANSPORT

I n the period covered by this book, both Keynsham and Saltford have grown, almost beyond recognition. Phases of house building have led to enormous increases in both population and area. To illustrate this growth, we look at aspects of development and the provision of public transport which, until the 1960s, was an essential part of almost everyone's life.

HOUSING IN THE EARLY POST-WAR PERIOD

The first general obligation on local authorities to provide housing was imposed by the Housing Act, 1919. Between the First and Second World Wars Keynsham Urban District Council had built some eighty council houses, but with the coming of peace again in 1945 an exhibition of development plans for the district, which included the provision of 250 new council houses, was mounted in October. The ten-year plan envisaged a doubling of the current population of 4,500 by 1953, and a possible population of 30,000, at a density of 3.5 persons per family, in twenty years.

While this was an expression of civic ambition, the realities of shortages of fuel, labour and materials were soon in evidence. Although work was in hand on the new Manor Road estate in Saltford by the end of 1945, in December there were appeals for householders to offer their spare rooms

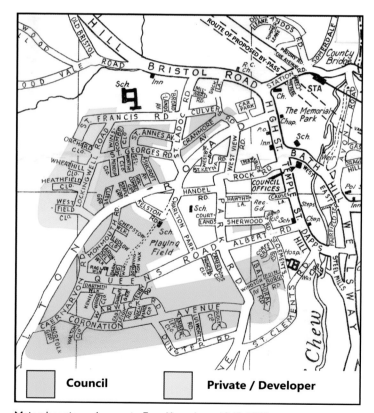

Major housing schemes in East Keynsham 1945-1960

Council   Private / Developer

to families who were homeless, or living in overcrowded conditions, or were returning service personnel. In order to reconcile needs

The Park Estate included several blocks of flats, mostly of three storeys such as this.

and resources, the Ministry of Health and Housing set up a national system of licensing for housing.

In June 1946, there were 541 families on the Council waiting list, despite the district having escaped essentially unscathed from war damage. As economic realities pressed, the Ministry announced that no licences for private building were to be granted, and temporary housing - in the form of 'pre-fabs' - began to be built: there were twenty locally by the end of 1946. During that year, in Keynsham, the site for the 54-house Culvers Road development was cleared, and approval sought for the Broadlands No 1 development of 82 houses, which extended the pre-war development on St Ladoc Road and St George's Road.

Despite the severe snows, which started on 21 January 1947 and effectively shut down most building sites, by April 1947 the number of new houses completed and occupied had reached fifty, and tenants' committees for each site were being encouraged.

Reviewing progress a year later, Council Chairman Edward Cannock lamented that the housing programme had been reduced to a mere shadow of actual requirements. For 1949, the Ministry's allocation for the district was just 33 houses (including only one by private enterprise). Strong objections to the Ministry were later rewarded by a supplementary allocation of 25 houses, justified by the UDC's intention to let the majority of new homes to key workers employed by local firms.

This early post-war period was very difficult for builders, with severe shortages of both labour and materials, especially timber; many projects took far longer than planned. In December 1945 the Council had sought approval for the builders to use Prisoners of War, though in the event this did not happen. Central government encouraged the development of pre-fabricated houses, both to use less labour and less timber. Over the next few years, many designs were promoted and the UDC built pre-cast concrete properties of the Unity design in Keynsham and by Woolaway in Saltford.

In 1949, there were still over 450 families on the waiting list, but by 1950 matters were at last improving, with the 164-home Broadlands scheme nearing completion, and planning well-advanced for the Norman Road scheme in Saltford. At Broadlands, the Council was keen to include several shops on the corner of St Ladoc

One of the most distinctive house designs used on the Park Estate was the 'Cornish', as on Coronation Avenue

Road and St George's Road but the Ministry did not agree to this. The quotas for 1951 were higher: 62 new council homes and, in a slight relaxation, nine by private enterprise.

A change of government brought the easing of restrictions and there was a huge expansion of local authority development. The Council looked east of Charlton Road and bought up agricultural land in the Park Road area. As an example we have details of a parcel of land, which included a house known as The Cameroons. This area of eleven acres, to the south of existing houses in Albert Road and Queens Road, belonged to the Heal family; they sold it to the Council in 1952 for £8,258 and it was developed in stages to include Windsor Avenue, part of Park Road and Berkeley Gardens. The original name is remembered in Cameroons Close.

In 1953, the UDC was approached by Bristol City Council, who were short of land on which to expand their housing stock. This Bristol 'Overspill' scheme was agreed by the end of the year, with a total 600 houses and flats to be built in Keynsham (more were added later), provided that seventy of them were allocated to families on the local waiting list. As the map shows, this increased the size of Keynsham enormously, and building took place from 1954 to 1959 between Park Road, Dunster Road and Charlton Road; it was named the Park Estate.

The houses built under these schemes were of various types but, compared to more recent designs, these 1940s and 1950s houses had good-sized rooms and generous gardens. Since the 'right-to-buy' legislation of 1980, many have become privately-owned, leading to improvements and alterations that give more individuality to their appearance.

By the mid-1950s, the house-building industry had expanded and materials shortages were a thing of the past. Private housing grew rapidly and east of the Chew this is when the lower part of Chandag estate was built; in west Keynsham, the Lockingwell Road area was developed about the same time. By 1961 the population of Keynsham reached 12,108 but growth continued. To the south of Coronation Avenue, the development by Federated Homes, comprising some 500 properties, took place in the 1960s. Together with the building of the Lays Drive scheme about 1971, this marked the limit of this side of the town for many years.

DEVELOPMENT IN SALTFORD

In modern times Saltford has been a predominantly residential area. In the years before 1939, the village had begun to increase in size as new houses were built around the old High Street area. Along the main A4 road, houses spread from the shops to opposite the Crown Inn and up Tyning, Rodney and Manor Roads. The village was part of Keynsham Urban District and in 1946, after the war, the Council was restricted by central government regarding the number of houses it could approve. There were many young families needing to be housed, but progress was slow. Council housing received most of the allocation and the designs were for good-sized houses and included a lot of green spaces.

As part of the initial post-war drive to provide more houses, 'temporary' prefabricated bungalows were built throughout the country and ten were completed in September 1946 on Lansdown Road; they have since been replaced. The development at Haselbury Grove, off Manor Road, was built at this time, while plans drawn up in 1944 for a development of some ninety houses in the Norman Road area were being refined. The artist's impression shows what was envisaged in 1946. The reality was somewhat less spacious and proved difficult to achieve. Shortage of materials and labour led the Government to promote pre-fabricated houses.

In 1950 and 1951 the Council awarded contracts to build about eighty houses on the Norman Road/Stratton Road development, of which twenty were of the Woolaway prefabricated pattern.

Construction of some of these was delayed when the builder ran into financial problems and eventually went into liquidation; the scheme was completed at the end of 1952 and included the spacious Broadway, leading to the future Community Hall. After completion of

NORMAN ROAD HOUSING SITE

Houses in Stratton Road, completed in 1952

Wedmore, Chelwood and Brockley Roads, the first accommodation for the elderly, consisting of small bungalows and a communal room with a warden, was built in 1961 at Wick House Close. This was followed soon afterwards by Iford Close, which incorporated a Community Room.

Eventually the government restrictions on private development were relaxed and in 1960 major development south of the A4 took place when Uplands Road, Uplands Drive, with Somerville Close and Beresford Close near the edge of the golf-course, were built. In 1961, the new Infant and Junior School was built in Claverton Road, providing capacity for development yet to come.

The largest expansion of Saltford took place from 1969 onwards, with the construction of

An unusual event around 1965, when precast concrete roof-sections from a modern house had to be removed, as the weight was causing the walls to bow

private housing on the Manor Lawns estate beyond the school to the west, followed by the Admirals' Park estate beyond, filling in the land across to Grange Road and linking Claverton Road to Claverton Road West. These two developments added about 350 houses to the Saltford property stock and played a part in raising the population of the village from 3,044 in 1961 to 4,080 thirty years later. Although the size of the development was substantial, the only provision for any community facilities was one or two areas of green space and a childrens' play area. However, many old footpaths were preserved in the various housing schemes and these provide valuable safe links between parts of the village.

The extent of building takes the village up to the boundary of designated Green Belt and no substantial developments have taken place since the end of the 1970s, although over the years infill development has occurred on many small plots, both in the old village and further out around The Folly and The Glen down Saltford

Hill. Planning applications that would extend the edge of housing to the north of Manor Road have been resisted and at 2020 there are no plans to enlarge the village.

Aside from housing, there have been changes in Saltford in the post-war period, although the number of employers has always been small. The riverside location has always been a factor in most local enterprise. In 1948, 68 people were recorded as working locally in 'Engineering & Industry', although this may have included some travelling to Keynsham. Taylor's Paints, at the former Saltford Mill on Mead Lane, employed 21 and the garages several more. Taylor's is believed to have closed about 1962 and after twenty years as a site for manufacturing Vermipeat – a soil-free compost invented by Hugh Folliott – the premises was sold to Saltford Pottery and became home to several artisan businesses. Thomas's Garage on the A4 was developed into a large showroom branded as Saltford Motors with a ramp into the workshop below, supporting its dealership for Vauxhall Motors.

In the 1980s, Wessex Water became the largest employer in the village when their scientific laboratory on Mead Lane was gradually expanded to become the organization's main centre for analysing water samples. At its maximum, this had about seventy staff, though this was later reduced as a result of increased

Saltford Marina in 2019

automation.

The attractiveness and accessibility of the riverside setting has made Saltford a centre for boating of various kinds. Boat building, hire, rowing, yachting and just enjoying the riverside have provided employment and pleasure over the years. Various establishments have come and gone in the post-war period, with Sheppard's Tea Rooms well-established for many years and replaced eventually by licensed premises, currently known as the Riverside Inn. A little further upstream, Saltford Marina was opened in 1986 and provides berths and support facilities for some 85 boats.

Other than changes to retail and leisure premises there has been little recent change in employment opportunities in the village. As

Sheppard's Tea Rooms in 1975, after closure

elsewhere, more people now work from home and the creation of the Community Post Office and Library in 2018 has provided a new focus for village life.

BUS SERVICES

In relation to their size and population, Keynsham and Saltford are quite well-served by bus services, with routes to a variety of destinations. This, in no small measure, may be attributed to the very early establishment of motor bus services by transport pioneers who chose Keynsham among other locations for early experiments, followed in February 1906 by the inauguration of a service between Brislington and Saltford on what is now the A4 road. Some sixty-five years earlier, the Great Western Railway had already begun to change travel patterns forever with its line adjacent to this highway. However, the tramways of Bristol (which reached Brislington; then still in Somerset, during late 1900) and Bath (to Newton St Loe in 1905) brought Keynsham and Saltford ever closer to these cities. While proposals to eventually connect these tramways failed to progress, the Bristol Tramways company was already conducting motor bus trials from Brislington to Keynsham and Burnett and shortly afterwards, commenced a service to

After the 1968 flood, buses were temporarily diverted along the Keynsham by-pass and access was allowed for passengers. This Bristol-bound bus on Route 339 pauses at a temporary stop.

Saltford and later Newton, to complete the link.

Services were suspended during the First World War but by the 1920s buses from Keynsham reached all the way to central

Bristol. The 1930s saw a full bus service between Bristol and Bath, while a second route from Bristol reached beyond Burnett to Paulton and Radstock.

Bristol Tramways had gained control of Bath Tramways by the 1940s, with motor buses taking over completely from trams in both cities. During 1944, a year before the end of the Second World War, the company

A cold wait for commuters outside the Lamb & Lark on 28 December 1962

started to adopt a new livery of Tilling green with cream relief, to replace its previous blue and white colours, or the dull grey applied in wartime.

Bus travel generally peaked in the fifties; thereafter, increased car ownership and the advent of television began to alter travel habits. Through Keynsham, the 1950 timetable shows the main Bristol-Bath route, No 33, offered a ten-minute frequency in each direction. In addition, service 88 ran roughly every half-hour from Bristol, through Marksbury to Radstock, with service 136 operating beyond Radstock to Frome. Over the river into Gloucestershire, service 303 connected Somerdale and Willsbridge every half hour, extending beyond to Warmley and Kingswood every hour. A substantial number of additional works services also developed to serve Fry's - with the drive at Somerdale lined with bus shelters to cater for demand.

A single decker, built by Bristol Commercial Vehicles and designed to be operated without a conductor, on the 349 route in Temple Street, October 1972

During the early 1950s, service 88A had been added to link Keynsham with Pensford and Whitchurch and by 1961, Pensford was also served via Queen Charlton twice daily by Service 33B. The number 33A had already been allocated a few years before to a new 30-minute service to Park Estate from Bristol. Meanwhile, Chandag Road was served hourly by route 301 to and from the Church.

A major regional route renumbering

A Bristol-built double decker at Keynsham Church on the service to Bath, with Old Vicarage Green under construction, in October 1972

exercise occurred in 1966 which saw the Bristol-Bath route become 339; service 349 served Park Estate and Chandag Road; Radstock services became 365/7, and those to Willsbridge and Hanham were numbered in the 380 series.

Bristol Tramways was among many transport concerns to be nationalized in 1948, and from 1957 changed its name to Bristol Omnibus Company. Twelve years later control passed to National Bus which led to the introduction of a lighter green corporate livery, but from the mid-1980s bus services were privatized and deregulated. For the Bristol and Bath areas, this saw Badgerline take over former Bristol Omnibus services, with buses now turned out in a bright yellow and emerald green, while other operators could now enter the market to compete. A number of service adjustments followed including many 339s becoming X39s and running via the Keynsham by-pass to provide a faster Bristol-Saltford-Bath link. Keynsham town, nevertheless, remained well served and new operations included local minibus services, including those of Norman's Coaches, trading as Merry-Go-Round, which lasted until 1993. Two years earlier, Alan Peter's Abus service commenced and, in 2020, still operates some services on the 349 Bristol - Park Estate service.

In 2013, another local concern, Bath Bus Company (whose depot is at Burnett) introduced a Bath – Saltford – Keynsham – Bristol Airport service which also caters for local passengers and which re-introduced Tilling green as its fleet colour.

Other local operators have also appeared, sometimes supported by the local council to encourage essential services, while the Badgerline operation became subsumed into transport giant First during the late 1990s.

A Badgerline Minibus, based on a Ford Transit chassis, similar to those used in Keynsham after 1986.
Photo © Geoff Sheppard Wikimedia Commons

At the time of writing, in 2020, there has been another renumbering of services, with the 339 becoming 39 and the 178 re-routed a couple of years ago to leave Chandag estate served only by local authority supported services. Nonetheless, in Keynsham and Saltford a good network remains with increased co-operation between companies, although traffic reduction schemes in Keynsham High Street concern the bus operators.

And this isn't quite the full story, as Bristol Commercial Vehicles of Brislington, which had earlier been part of the Bristol Tramways concern, followed those very early motor trials by not only building its own buses for local use,

In March 2016, outside Keynsham Church, a Bath Bus Company Volvo heads for Bath on the appropriately numbered A4 service.

but expanding to supply bus operators in every corner of the UK, and some abroad. Brand new 'Bristol' built buses became a familiar sight in Keynsham, often in bare chassis form, as the company's test route brought them through Keynsham, along the Wellsway to Burnett, then on to Chelwood before returning to Brislington via the A37 Wells Road. Almost every 'Bristol' bus undertook this journey prior to delivery, until closure of the works in 1983. In total, some 37,000 'Bristol' buses were produced over a 75-year period.

RAILWAYS

Norman Bartrum – Keynsham's last Station Master, who had the role from 1952 until 1965.

One of the last steam-hauled trains for Fry's employees empties at Keynsham & Somerdale on 11 June 1963

Throughout the Second World War, the railways were the arteries of the nation. Freight took precedence over passengers and maintenance was reduced to essential work only, so that when peace came in 1945 the system was generally run down. Between Bristol and Bath, the timetable was soon restored to its pre-war pattern. Ownership of private cars was the preserve of a small minority so that commuting into Keynsham for Fry's was mainly by train and residents travelled to Bristol and Bath by train or bus.

On a typical weekday some 26 trains in each direction stopped at Keynsham, then known as Keynsham & Somerdale. Of these, several were provided specifically to bring workers from different stations in Bristol to the Fry factory and some of these terminated at Keynsham. Compared to today, there was a more limited range of destinations with half the eastbound trains running just to Bath and almost all the westbound ones terminating at Bristol. In the early 1950s there were two trains a day to Portsmouth and one to Reading via Devizes. At this time Saturday morning was part of the normal working week, so the Saturday timetable had lunchtime trains to take Fry's workers back to Bristol. Sunday

Saltford Station and goods yard 10 November 1956

services were much reduced with only about ten trains in each direction. As new housing was built in Keynsham, more workers moved from Bristol. Other, newer, staff tended to live further away from the railway and travelled by bus. Both factors reduced demand for the workers' trains so the number provided gradually decreased through the 1960s. By 1974 there was just one morning train from Clifton Down that terminated at Keynsham.

In the 1950s local freight was a major part of the railway's activities and almost all substantial industrial concerns were connected to the railway and had their own sidings. Small businesses were served by the local goods yard and both Saltford and Keynsham stations had these until 1959 and 1965 respectively. As well as the connection across Station Hill into Fry's there were, at different times, private sidings into the ES & A Robinson paper mill and three other businesses. When colour-light signalling was

installed in 1969 the track layout was simplified by removing the connections to these sidings.

The immediate post-war period saw the railways still a major employer and even small stations such as Keynsham required station staff, signalmen, goods yard clerks, workers and delivery drivers. The station was a centre for other businesses such as coal merchants who worked out of the goods yard and the livestock dealers who used the railway to move cattle and sheep to and from Keynsham Market until the late 1950s.

A regular sight on Station Hill, Keynsham - the Fry's shunter crosses the road in 1977

On 1 January 1948, the railways were nationalized and the Great Western Railway, after 115 years, ceased to exist, becoming the Western Region of the new British Railways. Apart from cosmetic changes, the immediate effects locally would have been few as far as the passengers were concerned. However, the next twenty years saw enormous changes to local train services, arising not from state ownership but from increasing prosperity and technological progress. The population of Keynsham was increasing rapidly, from 6,349 in 1951 to 12,108 in 1961, and car ownership rose steadily.

A big change took place in 1959. Steam locomotives hauling trains of coaches with separate compartments and no connecting corridor were replaced on almost all local services by new diesel trains - more comfortable, quicker and cleaner. Passenger numbers had been falling everywhere and there was a real hope that the new trains would attract more custom; a large investment was made to provide a new timetable with 34 trains each way stopping at Keynsham.

However, the optimism was misplaced and within three years the Western Region cut more than one in three trains across the Bristol area. Keynsham now had eighteen weekday trains in each direction, still including two trains for Fry's staff, and Sunday services ceased. Usage continued to fall; in June 1968 only about 120 return journeys a week were being made from the station (and most of these were on the four Fry's trains) and in the following October formal notice of closure of Keynsham Station, along with many others on the line to Weymouth, was given.

After a campaign against closure, the Minister of Transport decided that peak-hour services should be maintained so the timetable in January 1970 was reduced to five trains per day in each direction and two on Saturday. The reprieve did not extend to Saltford Station, which had generally been served by the same

A diesel unit between Keynsham and Saltford in May 1964 Photo © Michael Mensing

A local tradition was an annual Sunday School outing to Weston-super-Mare. In the 1950s the churches combined for this; here is the scene of expectation at Keynsham station on 19 June 1961, the penultimate year that this event took place.

trains as Keynsham, and it closed on 5 January. During the following year the station buildings at Keynsham were demolished and the footbridge dismantled to be sold to the Dart Valley Railway in Devon. The 1970s proved to be the nadir of the station's fortunes. Avon County Council was created in 1974 and, after a period to become established, began to take a wider view of transport provision in the area. Road congestion was forcing more commuters onto the trains and by 1982 a few additional services were being provided. In 1985, the County Council part-funded the new footbridge and construction of the car park. More trains were being provided and Keynsham became a stop on the Portsmouth Harbour to Cardiff route, seeing ten services a day to the south coast in 1988.

Management of the railways saw its next major upheaval in 1996, when privatization became effective. The functions of British Railways were split between different companies and most train services to Keynsham were operated by one company – initially Wales and West – while the expresses passing through to London were operated by another – First Great Western. From 2006 almost all the services were within the same franchise and operated by First Great Western. The new arrangements meant that train services and details such as the number of coaches were effectively fixed for several years, so when passenger numbers increased there was no flexibility to add more trains or more coaches. Overcrowding on the peak-hour services between Bath and Bristol was nothing new but it became more frequent. On the other hand, new routes were introduced providing through trains to London Waterloo and Worcester as well as the Cardiff and south coast services that already existed.

Recent years have seen the number of trains serving Keynsham increasing at each timetable review, so that in January 2020 there were 29 to Bath and 31 to Bristol on a typical weekday, with at least one train every hour, while weekend services have improved also. Keynsham Station was seeing more business than at any time since the mid-fifties: in 2015-2016 the number of journeys starting or finishing at the station was estimated at 424,000 and by 2018-2019 this had risen to 511,600 – a far cry from the equivalent figure of about 12,000 in 1968. As well as significant new housing in Keynsham, some of which is very close to the station, the regeneration of the Somerdale site has brought several hundred jobs and in 2020 the station is once again seeing commuters arriving, as well as travelling out to Bristol and Bath.

In 2015 and 2016, the line through Saltford

Works at Keynsham Station in April 2016

Passengers board a train to Weymouth at Keynsham on a snowy day in March 2018

and Keynsham saw significant improvement works carried out by Network Rail, preparatory to the electrification announced in 2011. Compounds were established at Saltford and Pixash Lane. In April 2016, the line was closed for a week to enable the track at Keynsham to be lowered at a reputed cost of about £3m. In the following November, it was announced that the electrification had been deferred indefinitely, so that local trains will remain diesel-powered for the foreseeable future.

ACKNOWLEDGEMENTS

This content of this book has been structured, researched and written by a group of members of the Society plus other volunteers with an interest in local history. Over the several years of work, members of the group have varied, although many have remained throughout. We are grateful to them all for their time, effort and commitment. Core contributors have been Gill Clark, Jill Coles, Richard Dyson, Joan Ellison, Sue Hopkins, Tony Mitchell, Phil Robbins, Hilary Smedley and Liz Walker, who between them have written most of Part 1 and the Local Personalities chapter of Part 2. We also acknowledge the contributions of Fiona Burchard, Shirley Janes, Peter John, Bob Porton, Diane Riley and Bridget Wells. Written sources include articles in many issues of the Society Journal and we acknowledge the authors of these. Editing has been undertaken by Richard Dyson, who appreciates the co-operation of all contributors in agreeing to their drafts being variously shortened, amended or lengthened to suit the requirements of space and consistency of style.

PART 1 – THROUGH THE YEARS

We do not have space for separate attributions for each year but thank the core contributors named above, with Gill Clark putting together the history of Fry's and Somerdale, and we appreciate the invited contributions from Alan Walker (Bonzo Dog Band), John Aldridge (Manor Road Woodland) and George Colbourne (Fry's Sentinel).

   We have been supported through checks on accuracy and approval to use content by representatives of many organizations and subjects, and the families of individuals featured, including John Aldridge, Mary Burnard, Hazel Cannock, Richard Canter, Jack Carpenter, Ian Carter, Ric Davison, Simon Day, Hugh Evans, Wendy Harwood, Mike May, John Pascoe, Tony Pascoe, Richard Ryan, SAMA 1982, Tricia Scammell, Joan Vince and Brian Vowles.

PART 2 – LIVES AND TIMES

The principal authors of these chapters, including some invited contributors, are:

CHAPTER 1

Local Personalities: As previously stated, with information and consents from the families of Percy Baker, Geoff Mabbs and Lilian Slade.

CHAPTER 2

Changing Face of Keynsham Shops: Phil Robbins, Richard Dyson.

CHAPTER 3

Education and Health. Primary and Secondary Education: Tony Mitchell. Saltford Primary and Adult Education: Hilary Smedley. Healthcare GPs: Hilary Smedley. Dental Services: Hilary Smedley. School Dental Service: the late Fred Smedley.

CHAPTER 4

Local Sports Clubs. Saltford Golf Club: Jill Coles. Keynsham Bowling Club: Jill Coles, Ian Tweedie. Keynsham Cricket Club: Phil Robbins, David Whittington, Derek Joyce. Keynsham Town FC: Jill Coles, Martin Coles. Keynsham Rugby Club: Jill Coles, Phil Robbins, Ian Tweedie. Keynsham Amateur Swimming Club: the late Jean Findlay, Thelia Beament.

CHAPTER 5

Places of Worship in Recent Times: Gill Clark.

CHAPTER 6

Housing in the Early Post-War Period: Peter John, Phil Robbins, Richard Dyson. Bus Services: Martin Curtis. Railways: Richard Dyson.

The Society is grateful for the contribution to the costs of this publication made by I J McGill Transport Ltd of Keynsham.

PICTURE CREDITS

We are grateful for permission to reproduce the images used in this book and listed below, as identified by page number. All images are ©. Photographs not attributed are © Keynsham & Saltford Local History Society or © Richard Dyson, except for a very small number where we have been unable to trace the owner of the copyright.

INDEX